Juliet Hacking

Princes of Victorian Bohemia

Juliet Hacking

Princes of Victorian Bohemia

Photographs by David Wilkie Wynfield

Prestel
Munich · London · New York

National Portrait Gallery

Front jacket: D.W. Wynfield, *William Swinden Barber* (fl. *1855–1898*), undated (1860s), see p. 53
Back jacket: D. W. Wynfield, *John Everett Millais (1829–1896)*, undated, see p. 69

Library of Congress card number: 99-069075

Prestel Verlag
Mandlstraße 26
D-80802 Munich
Germany
Tel.: (89) 38-17-09-0
Fax: (89) 38-17-09-35

4 Bloomsbury Place
London
WC1A 2QA
Tel.: (171) 323 5004
Fax: (171) 636 8004

175 Fifth Avenue
New York
NY 10010
Tel.: (212) 627-9090
Fax: (212) 627-9511

Prestel books are available worldwide. Please contact your nearest bookseller or any of the above addresses for information concerning your local distributor.

Editorial direction by Philippa Hurd
Edited by Christine Davis
Designed and typeset by Matthias Hauer in Monotype Bulmer

Color separations by Fotolito Longo, Frangart/Bolzano
Printed and bound by Sellier, Freising

Printed in Germany

ISBN 3-7913-2301-6 (hardcover)
ISBN 3-7913-2359-8 (paperback)

Author's Acknowledgements

My heartfelt thanks to Pat Eaton and the staff of the Royal Academy Library, London; Pam Roberts and the staff of the Royal Photographic Society, Bath; the Design, Exhibition, IT and Publications departments of the National Portrait Gallery, London; and Philippa Hurd and staff at Prestel. I am also indebted to Liz Prettejohn, Caroline Arscott and Terence Pepper for respectively initiating, supervising and supporting my research on Wynfield.

Publisher's Acknowledgements

The quotation on the back of the hardback jacket comes from the Tennyson Research Centre, Lincoln and is reproduced by permission of Lincolnshire County Council.

Contents

Foreword

By contrast to the work of Julia Margaret Cameron, the photographs of David Wilkie Wynfield are not well known. Yet they are uncannily similar in both concept and composition: large-scale heads in poses which are wilfully historical, abstracted from the period in which they were taken and created to look as if their subjects have emerged from a Renaissance painting. To late twentieth-century eyes, they can appear over-theatrical, representing a group of artists with a false view of their own destiny. So much of twentieth-century photography concentrates on a much narrower view of the face, stripping it of any surrounding accretions in order to lay bare the personality of the person behind.

And yet, precisely because the photographs of David Wilkie Wynfield are so different in conception from any modern photograph, they challenge the viewer to ask questions about the circumstances in which they were created. The faces which look out from the garb of a Raphael or a Titian, a Rembrandt or a Hals are those of artists who were often to become well known in their later career, including, for example, George Frederic Watts and Frederic, later Lord Leighton. Moreover, bizarrely and unexpectedly, the group includes a fine photograph of the young Edouard Manet, not so self-conscious as his English contemporaries, but staring hard and dourly at the lens.

I am delighted that the National Portrait Gallery has been able to bring together these remarkable photographs. The exhibition will ensure that this aspect of its own collections of Victorian photography are properly studied and appreciated. But we are also greatly indebted to the Royal Photographic Society for lending Wynfield photographs not represented in our collection and especially so to the Royal Academy for its extremely generous loan which has enabled us to assemble the most comprehensive exhibition of his work since his lifetime. To both these institutions I wish to extend our wholehearted thanks.

In this excellent book which accompanies the exhibition Juliet Hacking helps to explicate Wynfield's milieu: the types of motives which led a group of young artists to dress up outrageously before settling down to a life of worldly and painterly success; and the attitude to art which retreated from nature as the touchstone of art to the belief that art should draw upon art itself. Just as the artists of the St John's Wood Clique drew upon the past in their paintings and drawings, so Wynfield dressed his sitters up in velvet or ruffs, plundering the language of past styles in a manner which is reminiscent of a certain tendency in late twentieth-century fashion. Indeed, it may be that it is the sensibility of designers such as Vivienne Westwood and John Galliano which makes these images appealing. For there is no reason why the photographer, like the fashion designer, should not plunder the dressing-up box of history in order to create a mood of wilfully archaic and nostalgic fiction.

Charles Saumarez Smith
Director, National Portrait Gallery, London

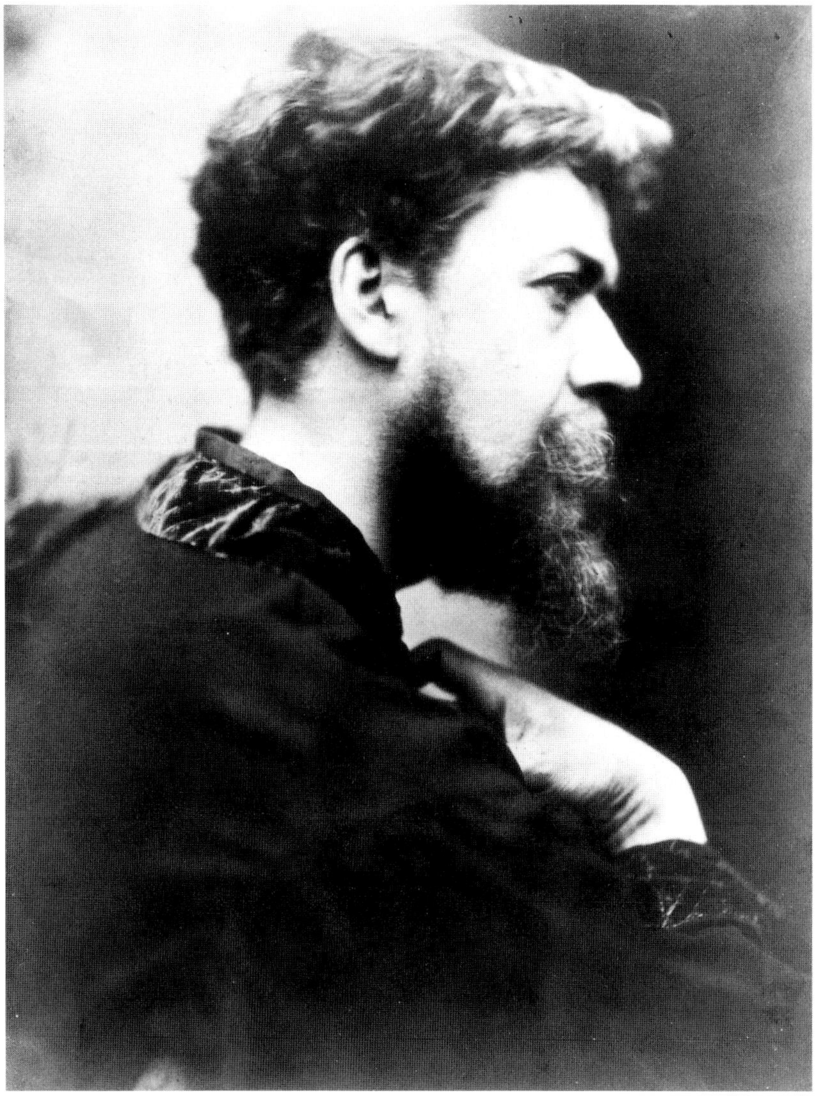

Hand and Soul
The Photography of David Wilkie Wynfield

The photographs made by David Wilkie Wynfield (1837–87), a member of the St John's Wood Clique or School of painters, have long remained an enigma. We know that he produced a number of distinctive bust portraits of artists in fancy dress in the mid-1860s but we do not know how or why he took up photography, who influenced him or the make of camera that he used. The Victorian mania for biography usually provides us with a rich vein of material to be examined. In Wynfield's case however there is only one extant letter by his hand, no diary or autobiography, and little more than passing references to his photography in the autobiographies or biographies of those who knew him well. His life almost makes a mockery of the biographer's tools: he was born in India a few months before the registration of births was introduced, he changed the spelling of his family name, he never married, he died at forty-nine without leaving a will. The most substantial collection of his photographs, that belonging to the Royal Academy in London, was locked away for most of the twentieth century. 'The lost pages of history' was how the art critic Francis Palgrave described the subjects painted by the St John's Wood Clique; the phrase could equally be applied to Wynfield's photographic career.

What is known, and widely repeated, about Wynfield as a photographer is that Julia Margaret Cameron, the most acclaimed British photographer of the nineteenth century, identified him as the dominant influence on her work. In a letter she wrote in 1864 Cameron told her friend Sir John Herschel, the eminent astronomer and photographic experimenter, that 'I have had one lesson from the great Amateur photographer Mr Wynfield & I consult him in correspondence whenever I am in a difficulty'. Two years later, shortly after her one-woman show at Colnaghi's, she chastised the art critic William Michael Rossetti for not visiting the exhibition and added in a postscript: 'Mr Wynfield too never went! & that surprised me. My Book there held the one great fact that to my feeling about his beautiful photography I owed all my attempts & indeed consequently all my success.' Cameron's debt to Wynfield is borne out by the evident similarities between the style, and occasionally the subjects, of their photographs (figs. 1 and 2). Nonetheless, whereas these accolades from Cameron are quoted or paraphrased in nearly every text which refers to Wynfield's photography they rarely appear in the abundant literature devoted to Cameron. Perhaps scholars are reticent to believe that a photographer about whom we know so little can really have made such a significant impact upon her work. The fact that there is so little evidence relating to Wynfield's photography is however no measure of his achievements. Cameron courted publicity and notoriety, Wynfield sought to evade them.

Although we do not know when Wynfield began making his portrait photographs we can pinpoint the moment at which he decided that they were worthy of public scrutiny. In December 1863 he registered for copyright ten portraits of artists in costume. The following month the 'Reports of Societies' columns in the photographic and periodical press noted

Left: D. W. Wynfield, *Self-portrait, profile*, undated (1860s), albumen print, 218 × 169mm, Royal Academy of Arts.

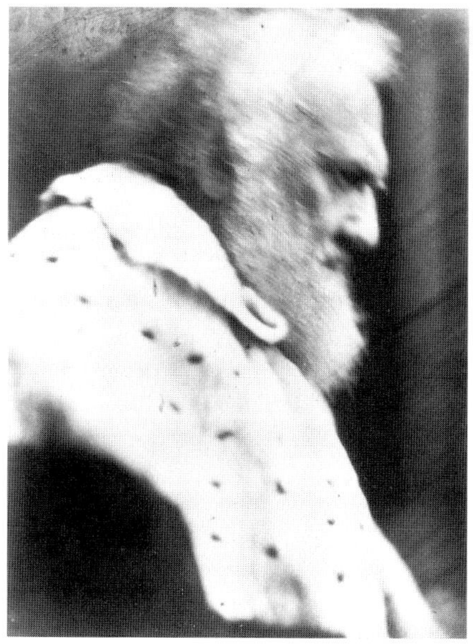

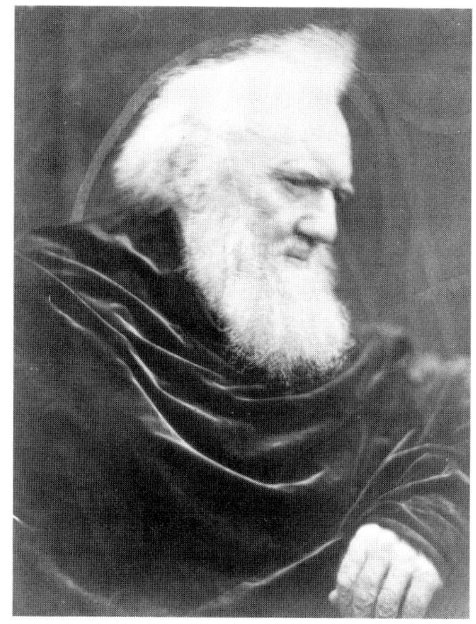

Fig. 1 D.W. Wynfield, *H. Thoby Prinsep*, undated (1860s), albumen print, 213 × 164mm, Royal Academy of Arts.

Fig. 2 J.M. Cameron, *H. Thoby Prinsep*, 1864, albumen print, 364 × 284mm, National Portrait Gallery.

that a number of photographs by him had recently been exhibited at the Graphic Society and at a meeting of the South London Photographic Society. Also in January 1864, an enthusiastic review of 'Mr Wynfield's Photographs' appeared in *The Reader*, a journal dedicated to science, literature and the arts. It is possible that this review persuaded Wynfield to publish his photographs; nonetheless, he chose to do so anonymously. By mid-March 1864 the first instalment of *The Studio: A Collection of Photographic Portraits of Living Artists, Taken in the Style of the Old Masters, by An Amateur*, was available from the photographic dealer Henry Hering of Regent Street. *The Studio* was mentioned in the *Illustrated London News* in March 1864, where it received a brief but laudatory notice, and in the *Art-Journal* in June, where it occasioned a few lines. It would appear that the publication was not a success and that, only six months or so after first exhibiting his photographs, Wynfield chose to withdraw them entirely from public circulation. A reviewer in *The Reader* noted with regret that he was not among the exhibitors at the tenth annual exhibition of the Photographic Society held in the summer of 1864. It was at this exhibition that Julia Margaret Cameron first exhibited her large-format bust photographs produced, claimed the critic of *The Reader*, according to 'Mr Wynfield's method' (*The Reader*, 4, p. 174). Cameron's photographs went on to become a *cause célèbre*; those of her so-called 'master', however, were soon forgotten.

Despite according him a place in the canon of important nineteenth-century photographers, Cameron's description of Wynfield as 'the Great Amateur' has contributed to the resilient identification of his photography as the dabblings of a dilettante. The members of the St John's Wood Clique were, like so many of their generation, addicted to amateur theatricals and fancy-dress parties and Wynfield's photographic portraits are often regarded as little more than an extension of these leisure activities. Such an assessment is in part a response to the fact that only a handful of his portraits have ever been exhibited or reproduced. In fact, over seventy different portraits by Wynfield of over fifty sitters have been preserved in British photographic collections alone. Both the consistency of treatment and the number of artists depicted suggest that the portraits form a related project. Although it is possible that they were intended for further instalments of Wynfield's 'Collection of Photographic Portraits of Living Artists' this does not account, however, for the small but significant exceptions to the widely held rule that he only photographed artists and always used costume. Wynfield not only photographed Thoby Prinsep (fig. 1), a retired civil servant, draped in an ermine robe, but also the historian James Anthony Froude (pl. 25) wearing a Puritan-style collar. Six of Wynfield's sitters do not wear historical costume and yet are portrayed in the same distinctive photographic idiom as those who do. One of these sitters is Edouard Manet (pl. 37). To discover that Manet, the avant-garde hero, sat for Wynfield, a member of a clique of artists whose name is synonymous with artistic compromise, is surprising indeed, not least because such a meeting defies conventional notions of aesthetic partisanship. No less surprising is the fact that, when the connections between Wynfield's sitters are examined in detail, it emerges that this was exactly what his photographic portraits were designed to do.

In bohemia with Du Maurier

Wynfield's series of bust portraits brings together a number of figures whom posterity has divided: artists such as John Evan Hodgson (pl. 4) and Edward Burne-Jones (pls. 30 and 31) are now polarised as representatives, respectively, of the establishment and the avant-garde. It also includes sitters who, although connected with the arts, were not 'artists' in the conventional sense: in addition to numerous painters Wynfield also photographed architects and graphic artists. Wynfield left no explanation of his aesthetic creed nor of the rationale behind his choice of sitters. Instead we are left to seek this rationale in the context in which the photographs were made and in the connections between the people that he chose to photograph. When he began to take photographs Wynfield was almost certainly in his twenties and working as a painter. His reputation, like that of most of his sitters, was yet to be made. For a brief moment the similarities between the conditions under which these men worked and the aspirations which they harboured were to be more significant than the aesthetic differences which would later come between them.

The majority of Wynfield's sitters were born in the 1830s, or the late 1820s; this is particularly the case with those who practised one of the arts. Those among this younger generation of

British artists who had studied or toured on the continent did not chose to remain there but instead returned to London to take advantage of the opportunities fostered by the expansion of the contemporary art market in the 1850s. This expansion led to a dramatic increase in the numbers entering the field and this in turn exacerbated the difficulties of making both a living and a name for oneself. There was however strength in numbers. Organising themselves into associations, clubs and coteries, this generation endeavoured to gain access to the established agencies of exhibition and criticism in order to promote the interests of themselves and their contemporaries. In addition to the professional societies such as the Artists' Society and Leigh's Sketching Club, which brought aspiring artists into contact with established ones, there were also the more select associations such the Medieval Society, the Hogarth Club, Morgan's in Berners Street and the Cosmopolitan Club, at whose meetings painters, engravers, designers and architects might rub shoulders with actors, writers, playwrights and journalists. When in 1862 George Du Maurier wrote to his friend Tom Armstrong that in London he would 'live entirely among artists', he used the term 'artist' to mean all the various bohemian types who populated the streets of the capital (*Letters*, p.181).

The letters written in the 1860s by Du Maurier (pl. 40) are an invaluable source for the period during which artists of Wynfield's generation identified themselves as brothers and not rivals. Prior to the 1860s, bohemia – that elusive realm populated by the young, creative and penniless – was not thought to exist outside of Paris. In 1863, however, Justin McCarthy noted that the writings of Thackeray, and in particular his novel *The Newcomes*, had brought bohemia to London. Nonetheless, McCarthy was at pains to point out the differences between the Parisian bohemia of Henri Murger, whose *Scènes de la vie de Bohème* of 1845 was still only available in French, and the London bohemia described by Thackeray. The latter, it would seem, was to be free of all the radical and immoral connotations of its French counterpart:

> The true Bohemia, must, above all things, be a region whose inhabitants are artists and live by art. Whatever the genuine Bohemian may be, it is absolute and essential that he must never be vulgar, and that he must always at least have the sympathies of a scholar and an artist, and something of the native grace of a gentlemen. Whoever would paint him must give him, under whatever circumstances, a dash of the picturesque.
> *Westminster Review*, 79, p. 50

It would appear that bohemia had lost something in the translation.

The notion that there were two types of bohemianism was central to *The Newcomes*. In the novel it is Clive Newcome's pure 'English' heart which allows him to mix at art school with representatives of the 'French' bohemian type, such as Fred Bayham, without being corrupted by their vulgarity and cynicism. Many of Wynfield's sitters, including Wynfield himself, trained at Leigh's, the art school which Thackeray attended as a young man, and the novelist's model of the respectable bohemian proved immensely significant for this generation. When at the end of the century Du Maurier came to write *Trilby*, the novel based on his experiences of training as an artist in Paris in the late 1850s, he made his English characters warm-hearted, loyal and gentlemanly in everything they said or did; their foreign counterparts, however, were not to be trusted. Such jingoistic sentiments appear ridiculous to the modern reader but we need to remember that for the Victorians 'French' did not simply designate a nationality but was also a euphemism for all that could not be said or done in polite society. For example, Du Maurier's letters reveal that he believed that he had two sides to his nature which were constantly at war with each other: a respectable, virtuous persona and a degraded one which sought gratification in alcohol and sex. The first he called his 'English' side, the second his 'French'. Du Maurier knew that if he was going to make a name for himself as an artist, his English side would have to get the upper hand.

In early 1864 Du Maurier wrote to Tom Armstrong:

> There is a man called Winfield Junior [sic], who has been taking large photographs of several of the fellows in 15 and 16 century costumes and they are splendid – you should see Lewis, Leighton, Calderon, Prinsep, Walker! Quel grands seigneurs!
> *Letters*, p. 228

Du Maurier's recognition of Wynfield's sitters as artist-princes owed much to the rhetoric which Thackeray used in *The Newcomes* to present the artist as the equal of nobility. When challenged by members of his family over his wish to become an artist, young Clive Newcome responds:

> Wasn't Reynolds a clipper! That's all! And wasn't Rubens a brick? He was an ambassador and a Knight of the Bath; so was Vandyke. And Titian, and Raphael, and Velasquez? I'll just trouble you to show me better gentlemen than them, Uncle Charles.
> *The Newcomes*, p. 137

Wynfield's generation had good reason to promote Old Master artists as the social equals of the patrons for whom they worked. The publication of *The Studio* came soon after the Select Committee enquiry of 1863 into the workings of the Royal Academy during which much of the discussion centred on the question of whether the artist was or was not a gentleman. The dilemma was that although works of arts were believed to enrich the soul they were also the product of manual labour. The artist worked with his hands whereas a gentleman never did.

Fig. 3 F. Walker, *Dear Arthur's Round Table*, 1866 (photograph courtesy of Witt Library, Courtauld Institute).

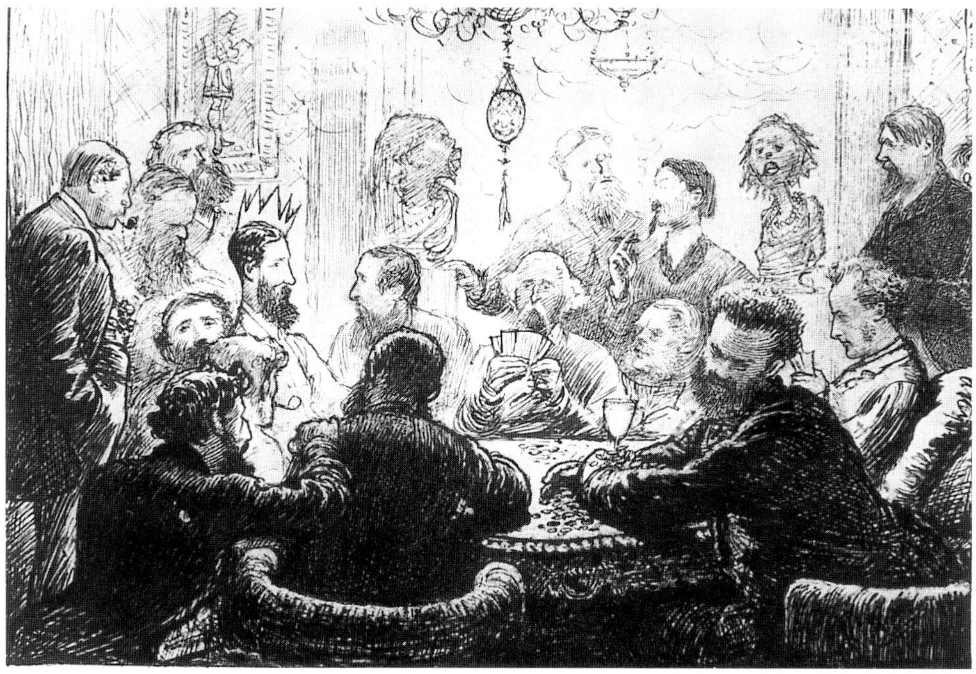

Whether or not he was a manual worker the artist certainly required the manners of a gentleman. In order to court patrons and influential supporters he had to leave bohemia – from time to time at least – and enter into London 'Society'. For some young artists their first invitation to a London salon came through the ties of kinship or friendship; for example, in the 1850s George Storey's friendship with George Leslie (pls. 6 and 7) saw him welcomed into the salon of his friend's father, the distinguished painter Charles Robert Leslie, in St John's Wood. Here Storey met, amongst others, Charles and Elizabeth Eastlake, Edward and Henrietta Ward, Tom Taylor, Edwin Landseer, Anna Jameson, Millais and Holman Hunt. Other aspiring artists gained entry to a salon by being noticed by an established member of the set and being introduced as a protégé. At receptions such as those at Little Holland House and the Denmark Hill home of the Ionides family, a controlled relaxation of the alienating rules governing social interaction was enacted in the name of art. Activities such as fancy-dress parties, musical soirées and amateur theatricals temporarily replaced the social hierarchy with one based upon talent, wit and invention. Nonetheless this new social order had its own unwritten rules: in his letters Du Maurier identified the moment at which Millais (pl. 27) acknowledged him socially as an indication of his increased professional standing. Those who craved success could not afford to become too closely associated with the bohemian life.

At Sara Prinsep's salon at Little Holland House the highest praise was reserved for men of letters and no artist was allowed to outshine the carefully tended genius of the artist-in-residence George Frederic Watts (pl. 35). It is no wonder that many young artists preferred to be entertained by another resident of Kensington, Arthur Lewis, the silk merchant and amateur artist (pl. 26). Frederick Walker's cartoon, *Dear Arthur's Round Table*, depicts this 'companion and friend of all the painters of his time, from Millais downwards' (*Pen and Pencil Sketches*, p.184) as a benign host surrounded by his loyal knights (fig. 3). Lewis's all-male 'bachelor' dinners and musical soirées came to an end in 1867 with his marriage to the actress Kate Terry. By this time, however, the homosocial network created by his patronage had been institutionalised in the shape of the United Arts Club, the idea for which originated at his Campden Hill home. At the Arts Club, as it quickly came to be known, this generation further indulged their pretensions to be modern-day knights. In 1869 the club's rooms in Hanover Square became the headquarters for the 38th Middlesex corps of the Artists' Volunteer Rifles, one of the hundreds of volunteer companies set up in the spring of 1860 when the aggressive expansionist policy of Napoleon III presented the threat of war with France. The ranks of this corps were, according to a contemporary notice, composed of 'painters, sculptors, engravers, architects, musicians, literary men, actors, amateurs, and gentlemen in any way interested in, or connected with, the arts'. Many of Wynfield's sitters (and all those in the Clique apart from George Leslie) were members of, or subscribers to, the corps: Charles Keene (pl. 11), Field Talfourd (pl. 22), George Price Boyce, William Swinden Barber (pl. 15), Carl Haag (pl. 21) and Joseph Jopling. Millais, Arthur Lewis, Frederic Leighton (pl. 34), Valentine Prinsep (pl. 33) and Henry Wyndham Phillips were among the first officers. In order to assume the honour of wearing the 'Queen's livery' the new recruit had to swear his allegiance to the monarch and to promise to defend her against all enemies. Wynfield's artistic brethren were also brothers-in-arms.

This patriotic fervour sits uneasily with the idea of the bohemian as the scourge of the establishment. However the young artist was required to slip between a number of contradictory guises in order to sustain the difference from others which would mark him out as an artist: he was to be both a naive sensualist and a man of the world, a talented natural and a perpetual student, a manual worker and a scholar. Shifting between these different guises had its benefits: it enabled the artist to sustain a social mobility that flouted convention and to court patrons from across the social and professional spectrum. In Wynfield's bust photographs this masquerade personality of the artist is conflated with the notion that a person's character was not fixed but instead a mixture of many traits, the different aspects of which would be revealed under changing circumstances. Wynfield's profile self-portrait (pl. 1), in which the diagonal lines of his profile are echoed by the position of his hand and the downward thrust of his arm, provides a dynamic contrast to his full-face self-portrait in which the prevailing mood is one of reflection (pl. 3). This is the artist as Renaissance courtier, moving between the *vita activa* and the *vita contemplativa.*

Mr Wynfield's method

Before Cameron's reputation eclipsed that of Wynfield, the 'out-of-focus' technique which became associated with her name was identified with his. I make this point not to diminish Cameron's achievements but to suggest that this identification was in part responsible for diminishing Wynfield's. The combination of soft focus, close-up, large-format whole-plate (8 × 6") print and historical costume produced a photographic idiom which was completely novel when Wynfield first exhibited his portraits in early 1864. In its review of *The Studio*, the *Illustrated London News* said of the portraits that:

> [they] possess greater softness, lifelike animation, and apparent power of movement, and breadth of light and shade than any photographic copies of pictures or studies from life we have ever seen.
> *Illustrated London News*, 44, no. 1250, p. 275

Despite assessing the works in this manner, the anonymous critic announced that he would not describe the portraits. Instead, he used them as a means to denigrate the commercial portrait photographer for his partiality to what was called 'a deathlike stillness and a universal distinctness'. Similarly, in *The Reader*'s review of *The Studio*, having acclaimed the images as 'the best portraits ever produced by means of photography' the critic went onto to insult the commercial portraitist (*The Reader*, 3, p. 145). It was alleged that the collapsing of social difference effected by 'common *carte* portraiture' was due to the fact that its practitioners were so vulgar as to be insensitive to the social distinctions between their sitters. These words incensed the self-styled champion of the would-be professional photographer, Alfred Wall, who wrote a series of articles in the photographic press in which he argued that a truly skilful photographer would use his technical expertise, and not 'masquerade costume', to create a good portrait. Wall implied that Wynfield's soft-focus style of photography was the result of ineptitude rather than a self-conscious attempt to make his photographs artistic. The association of Wynfield's name with the 'out-of-focus' technique secured a reading of his photographs as little more than an amateurish challenge to *carte-de-visite* portraiture.

By describing the appearance of Wynfield's photographs we can begin to identify other layers of meaning to them. Wynfield invariably posed his sitter in front of a background divided into indistinct areas of light and dark arranged in order to achieve a contrast to the white of the face and the dark of the hair. The costume worn by the sitter was also arranged to create contrasting areas of light and dark. The portrait of William Gale (pl. 9) is a particularly successful example. In this photograph, the area of shadowed background is paired diagonally with the dark-coloured cloak. These two patches of dark sepia are separated by the pale finger that extends to meet Gale's light-coloured shirt. The patch of light provided by the hand balances that behind Gale's head. Wynfield's use of an extremely narrow depth-of-field enabled him to work with chiaroscuro; areas of light and dark blend or blur into one another creating a fusion of background and subject. In this portrait the left-hand side of Gale's face is thrown into relief by the dark background and yet merged with it through the shadow around the eye area. The scattering of light rays across the glass plate effected by the use of an open aperture ensured that there were no dead shadows in this or any other of Wynfield's portraits.

The 'apparent power of movement' found in a number of Wynfield's portraits derives from the combination of the long exposures during which the sitter might move, and the narrow depth-of-field which suggests to the viewer's eye that the head of the sitter is about to move into the plane of focus. In his portrait of Richard Ansdell this effect is enhanced by the use of *contrapposto*, the muscular tension created by posing the sitter with his head facing away from his torso (pl. 14). The hand of the sitter often lends additional vitality to the portrait, a device that the critic of *The Reader* recognised as a reference to Van Dyck. What the critic did not recognise however was that the reference was as much conceptual as stylistic. It is likely that the model which Wynfield had in mind when he created *The Studio* was *The Iconography*, Van Dyck's series of engraved portraits of his contemporaries. Van Dyck's project was divided into three principal groups: artists and collectors; princes and military commanders; and statesmen and philosophers. (The first, and most substantial, group ran to fifty-two portraits.) The sepia tonality of Wynfield's photographs corresponds to the preparatory drawings for this series, a number of which were at this time in the collection of the Duke of Buccleuch at Montague House in Whitehall. The parallels between *The Studio* and *The Iconography*, and the fact that Wynfield chose to exhibit his works at the Graphic – rather than the Photographic – Society, suggest that he was seeking to situate his portraits in relation to graphic art rather than commercial photographic portraiture (fig. 4).

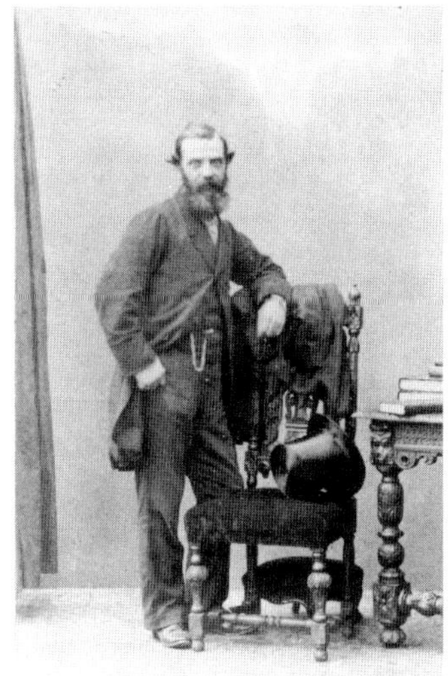

Fig. 4 Caldesi, Blanford & Co., *Richard Ansdell*, undated (1860s), albumen *carte-de-visite*, 87 × 56mm, National Portrait Gallery.

Past and present

Wynfield would probably have known of the preparatory drawings for *The Iconography* from Gustav Waagen's three-volume *Treasures of Art in Great Britain*. Published in the 1850s this work exposed the myth that the British had no tradition of collecting and connoisseurship. Waagen's work provided the impetus for the Manchester Art Treasures exhibition of 1857, the organisation of which took the visitor through the great continental schools of the past and concluded with British art of the present. Wynfield and his closest friends were at art school at the time of this reassessment of Britain's contribution to the arts and were anxious to play their part in it. In 1864 Francis Palgrave wrote:

> The [Royal Academy] Exhibitions of 1862 and 1863 showed there was a new rising school of young artists determined to prove themselves fit for public honour, and anxious to vindicate for English art that higher style and greater breadth of subject in which, it was felt, foreign artists had gained an advance upon our insular security.
> *Essays on Art*, p. 45

One of the reasons that Britain was believed to lag behind other European nations artistically was that British art showed no unity of style; there was no British 'school'. The rhetoric which emerged from the Manchester exhibition, however, claimed that the strength of British art was like the strength of the British constitution: it encouraged freedom of thought and action. Such patriotic sentiments were the foundation upon which the 'rising school' established their own style of art.

The celebration of artistic diversity was central to the art teaching of Charles Robert Leslie. In 1855 Leslie published as *A Hand-book for Young Painters* the lectures on art which he had given as professor of painting at the Royal Academy. Leslie strongly criticised partisanship in terms of artistic influence and promoted an approach which he identified variously as 'catholic' or 'eclectic', stating that:

> no painter of true taste can see an excellence anywhere, without the wish to engraft it on his own style. So it was with Raphael, with Titian, with Rubens, and with every painter of comprehensive mind.
> *Hand-book*, p. 37

This positive assessment of the eclecticism of the Old Masters was important for the artists of the 1860s who were looking to move contemporary art beyond Pre-Raphaelitism. The practice of sketching from a set subject from history, mythology or the Bible was the basis of the tuition provided both by Leigh's art school and the various sketching societies. It engendered a style of art that placed the qualities of invention and composition above those of finish. If these artists could secure an identification between themselves and their cultivated predecessors then this would serve them in their move away from 'the painstaking detail and fidelity to nature' of Pre-Raphaelitism, as George Leslie later called it, towards their own painterly idiom (*Inner Life*, p. 53). An appreciation of the Old Masters was to free them from a slavery to the 'Old Mistress', as Millais called nature.

The majority of Wynfield's costumed portraits refer to what was perceived to be the greatest period of royal and aristocratic patronage of the arts in Europe, the sixteenth and early seventeenth century, and specifically in the case of England the reigns of Henry VIII, Elizabeth I and Charles I. The stylistic borrowings from artists of this period tend to be from those, such as Holbein and Van Dyck, who worked as court painters. Natural sources of reference for works by such artists would have been the Royal Collection, many treasures from which were reproduced photographically in the 1860s, and the recently established National Portrait Gallery. Wynfield did not, however, seek to recreate specific works by Old Masters; his portraits are either 'in the manner of' a certain artist or combine a number of Old Master references in one image. For example, his use of foliage to break up an otherwise empty background was a borrowing from Holbein and yet he also used it in portraits in which the sitter is dressed in Florentine costume (pl. 34). The portraits make a series of generalising references and eclectic syntheses which were designed to identify Palgrave's 'rising school' as painters of 'true taste'.

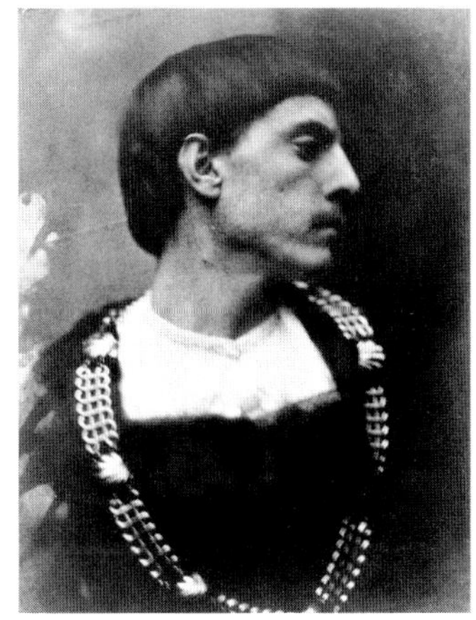

Fig. 5 D.W. Wynfield, *Frederick Walker, in profile*, undated (1860s), albumen print, 211 × 165mm, Royal Academy of Arts.

According to Dante Gabriel Rossetti's prose narrative *Hand and Soul*, to work for fame was anathema to the true artist. In Wynfield's bust portraits the desire for and the renunciation of fame is an abiding preoccupation. The series brings together artists such as Millais who had achieved recognition and those, like Wynfield himself, who courted it. In subjecting his sitters to a distinctive photographic treatment Wynfield identified them as united in their devotion to the advancement of art: for these artists individual fame is glory for all. Not a mechanical limner but a Renaissance man, the artist (of whatever shading) is the equal of nobility in his culture and learning. Gifted in the arts of battle as well as in the liberal arts, he is a knight loyal to his muse and to his monarch. To Du Maurier, Thoby Prinsep may have been 'the original of Old Newcome' (*Letters*, p. 119); in Wynfield's portrait series Prinsep in his ermine robe and Arthur Lewis in his courtly apparel are modelled in the image of men such as Thomas Howard, 2nd Earl of Arundel and Surrey, the connoisseur behind the introduction of distinguished foreign artists to the court of Charles I. According to *The Studio*, the artists of Britain were not seeking fame for its own sake but to make their nation once again a significant force in the arts.

Personal portraiture

When twentieth-century writers have sought the meaning behind Wynfield's use of costume they have assumed that it is more or less transparent. In 1927 Mary Stephen Smith, a niece of W.F. Yeames (pl. 8), identified the choice of costume as based upon physiognomic likeness:

> Working for his private satisfaction, Wynfield would take large portrait studies of friends whose faces interested him, invariably arranging some sort of head-dress or costume which he fancied suited the type of face. Thus in the portrait

Fig. 6 Unattributed photograph, *Myles Birket Foster, friends and family in costume*, (c.1864–6), reproduced in Jan Reynolds, *Birket Foster*, London 1984, p.118. Birket Foster stands behind the two seated women and Watson, in white, reclines on the ground.

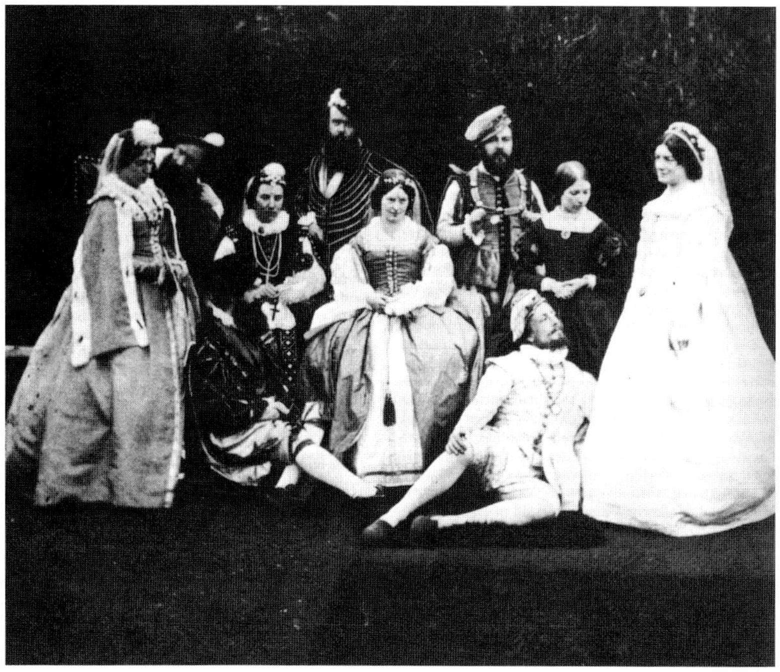

> of John Everett Millais, he produced the head of Dante; whilst from Frederick Walker's beautiful profile he evolved a young Florentine painter.
> *Art and Anecdote*, p. 152

In an article written in 1973 by Smith's own niece, the portrait of Frederick Walker in profile was again identified as representing a Florentine artist (fig. 5). Margaret Garner hesitated, however, when she came to discuss the portrait of Millais 'as Dante' 'to compare the painter of *Bubbles* with the author of *The Inferno* seems to be going a little too far' (*Apollo*, 97, p. 58). And indeed it does, that is unless the portrait is read as an identification between the crisp lines of Millais's profile and the precise draughtsmanship of fourteenth-century Florentine art. A central preoccupation for artists was the age-old question as to whether line or colour was the most important quality in a work of art. Artists who expressed a preference for one over the other usually divided themselves between an allegiance to the Florentine or the Venetian school. The eclectic art produced by Wynfield's generation, however, sought to find a balance between the two.

For this generation, an aesthetic appreciation of the Old Master style was conflated with an appreciation of the Old Masters themselves as ideal types of manly beauty. When Wynfield photographed John Dawson Watson in the manner of Van Dyck, the sitter's beard and whiskers were evidently primped in order to bring out a likeness between Dawson and his historical predecessor (pl. 42). We can deduce that Watson was proud of this resemblance from the photograph taken at Myles Birket Foster's home in Surrey of family and friends indulging in fancy dress (fig. 6). In this photograph both Watson and Foster wear costumes similar to those in which they were photographed by Wynfield (fig. 7 and pl. 19). These are not the only portraits by Wynfield for which the costume was more likely to have been suggested by the sitter than the photographer. In his full-face portrait of Frederic Leighton (pl. 36), the artist wears a costume which is almost identical to that seen on the male figure in Leighton's 1864 painting *Golden Hours* (fig. 8). In Wynfield's three-quarter profile of Leighton (pl. 34) the artist wears an elaborate white costume similar to that worn by Cimabue in Leighton's monumental canvas *Cimabue's Madonna is Carried in Procession through the Streets of Florence* (fig. 9). Leighton's desire to be recognised as the equal of this fêted artist was satirised by Du Maurier in his letters. Describing to his sister a soirée held at Abraham Solomon's in 1861, he wrote:

> Cimabue was there – I don't know whether you would like him, very blasé and finikin, and quite spoilt – one of the world's little darlings, who won't make themselves agreeable to anything under a duchess.
> *Letters*, p. 33

Du Maurier's satire was tinged with anxiety. By 1862 Leighton was one of the many painters who were encroaching on the graphic artist's domain. In October of that year Du Maurier complained to his mother that he was now competing with Leighton and 'other swells you have not heard of, who spare no expense in time, industry and models' (*Letters*, p. 170). It is no surprise that Du Maurier was happy to be made the equal of this 'swell' by sitting for Wynfield in armour (pl. 40).

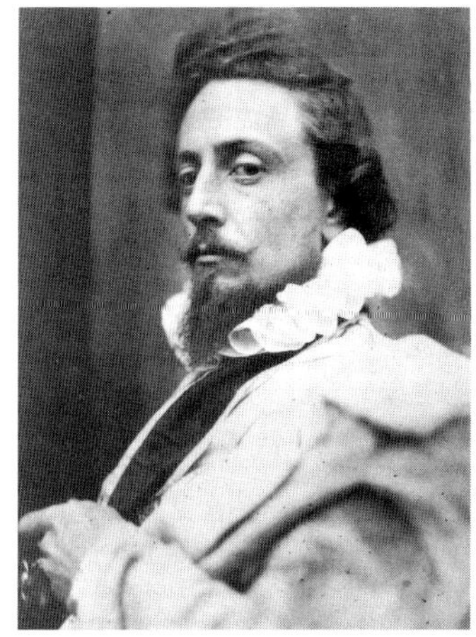

Fig. 7 D.W. Wynfield, *John Dawson Watson, wearing a ruff*, undated (1860s), albumen print, 262 × 210mm, National Portrait Gallery.

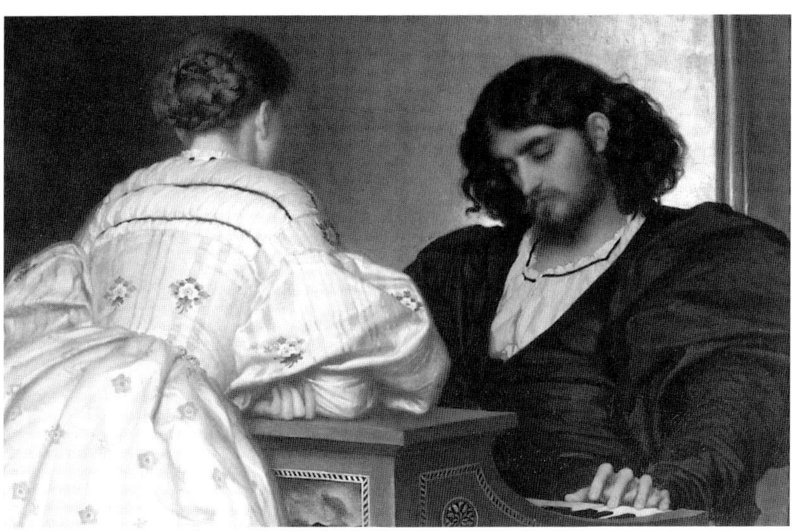

Fig. 8 F. Leighton, *Golden Hours*, 1864, oil on canvas, 915 × 1220mm, private collection.

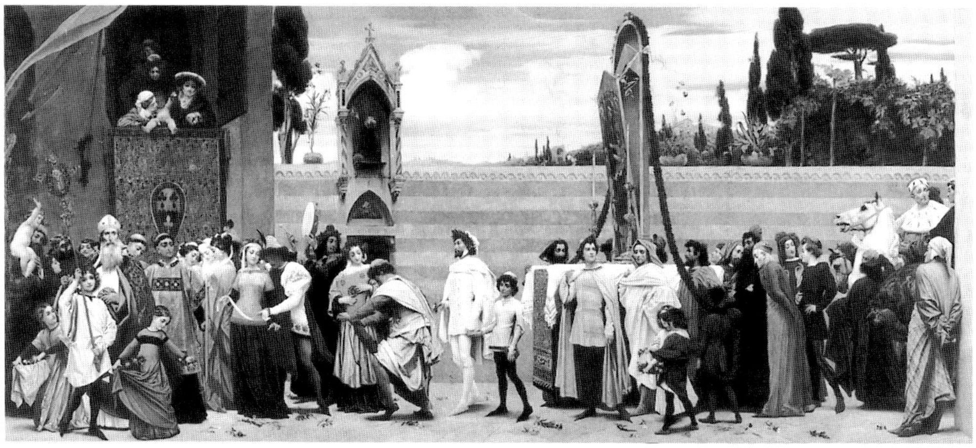

Fig. 9 F. Leighton, *Cimabue's Madonna is Carried in Procession through the Streets of Florence*, 1854–5, oil on canvas, 2317 × 5209mm, The Royal Collection.

According to 'A Brief Enquiry into the Portraiture of Historical Painting', an article published in the *Art-Journal* in early 1864, the ability of Old Master artists to recognise a correspondent beauty between their friends and family and that of the historical or Biblical figures that they wished to depict was a testament to the sublimity of their characters. 'Personal portraiture', as it was called by the *Art-Journal*, was practised widely by Wynfield's generation (in part, one suspects, because it gave a theoretical underpinning to the fact that friends came cheaper than professional models). The *Art-Journal* further asserted that the Old Masters were distinguished by their ability to represent the psychological complexity of their noble sitters. The suggestion that art was a revelation of the character of both sitter and artist was central to Gustav Waagen's theories of art. In the preface to the English translation of Waagen's *Peter Paul Rubens: His Life and Genius* of 1840, R.R. Noel wrote:

> What we call the style of a painter is not merely the manner in which he has executed with his pencil certain subjects, but the soul of a man made sensible to the reflecting and philosophical observer in the product of his hand.
> *Rubens*, p. viii

There can be little doubt that Wynfield's portraits were intended to function on one level at least, as psychological portraits. The critic in *The Reader* described the costumes seen in Wynfield's photographs as 'medieval', a term that had great currency in the period. It was commonly used to denote the subject matter of the writings of Tennyson, Keats and Browning, and that of the artists who were inspired by their poetry. It was also used by historicising artists and critics sympathetic to them to denote a sensibility which was thought to pervade the art and literature produced during the transition between the age of faith and the age of reason. The humanist philosophy of the sixteenth century which discovered in learning the means for man to intercede in his destiny suggested that the panacea to the recognition of one's own mortality was glory on earth as well as in heaven. The psychological trauma that this engendered, and which gave rise to the iconography of melancholy and *memento mori* images in the arts of the Renaissance, finds its parallel in the psychological condition that Wynfield's contemporaries identified as the affliction of their times: that of melancholy and morbidity, a state that was identified with a crisis, or loss, of faith.

In 1871 Tom Taylor wrote an account of Wynfield's art and career for *The Portfolio*, the art periodical established by Philip Gilbert Hamerton the year previously. In this account he noted that the episodes chosen by Wynfield for his historical tableaux frequently had a tragic element to them. There is also a tragic element to Wynfield's portrait photographs. The technical advances of the nineteenth century which increased at an accelerated rate man's knowledge of his world also stressed the insignificance of human life and endeavour in the face of the unceasing cycles of evolution and decay. By making reference to a previous age of transition Wynfield's portrait series highlights the psychological dilemmas engendered both by the condition of the Victorian age and by the artist's own condition: the transition from youth to maturity, nonconformity to conformity, faith to reason. When Wynfield's sitters assume meditative, melancholic expressions, look into the far distance or deep into the camera, the artist appears as both gifted and damned: gifted with the talents of his noble predecessors and damned by the awakening to the nature of the human comedy which attended the transition to both physical and artistic maturity.

Fig. 10 F. Walker, *A Dream of the Clique*, undated (c.1865), reproduced in M.S. Smith, *Art and Anecdote*, London 1927, p.142.

Fig. 11 D.W. Wynfield, *The St John's Wood Clique*, undated (1860s), reproduced in H.S. Marks, *Pen and Pencil Sketches*, London 1894, p.182.

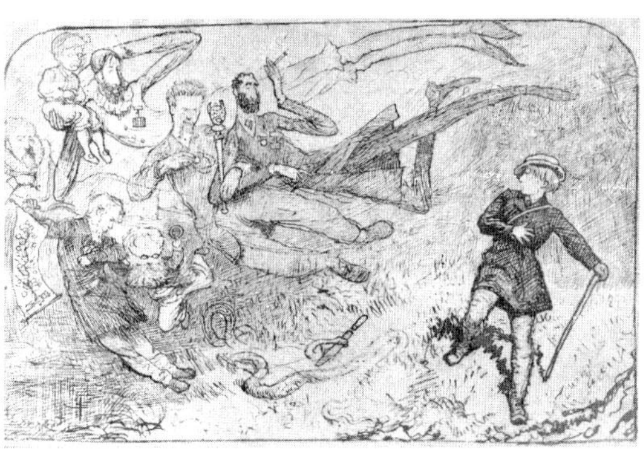

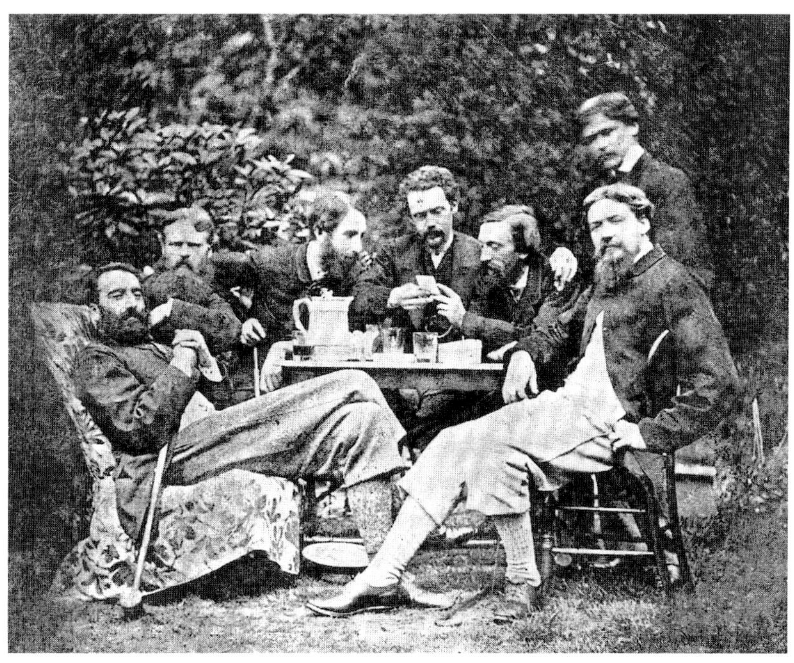

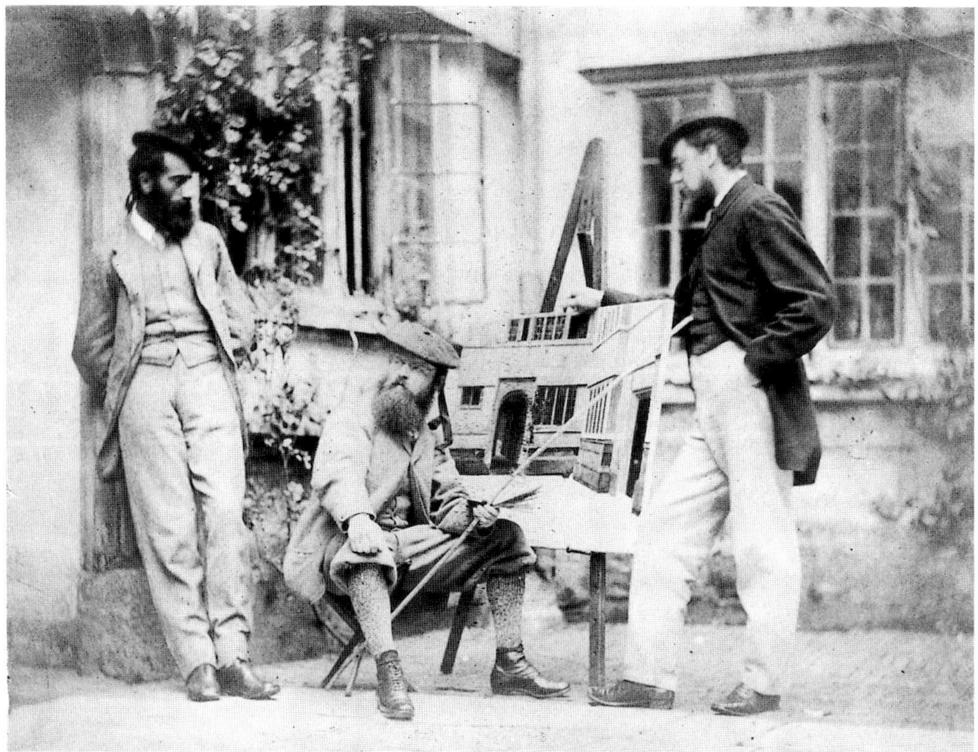

Fig. 12 D.W. Wynfield, *P.H. Calderon, W.F. Yeames and D.W. Wynfield at Hever Castle*, c.1866, albumen print, private collection.

In Frederik Walker's cartoon *A Dream of the Clique* (fig. 10) drawn in the mid-1860s, the artist distinguished himself from his contemporaries by emphasising his boyish appearance. At the end of the century Du Maurier used Walker as the model for Little Billee in *Trilby*, immortalising him as the man-child whose pure heart required protection from the cynicism of his peers. In Wynfield's full-face portrait of Walker the artist also personifies this man-child; he is no 'Florentine artist' but instead, as Bevis Hillier suggested, plays Hamlet (pl. 41). Wynfield sought to arrest his sitters at the moment at which youthful aspiration bound them to one another as brothers in art. His desire to do so suggests he knew that the fame they sought would divide them.

Sic transit

The popularity of the historical paintings of the St John's Wood Clique brought recognition to its members long before many of their contemporaries. In the mid-1860s these artists won the favour of influential patrons and came to command high prices for their works. It was in the wake of this success that the Clique began to forge a version of bohemianism that asserted their 'English' wholesomeness in the face of the 'French' inclinations of some of their peers.

Wynfield's group portraits of the St John's Wood Clique are usually reproduced as informal, documentary images; they are in fact carefully constructed images of respectable bohemianism (figs. 11 and 12). The interwoven poses and unconventional dress of the sitters serve to identify them as members of the brotherhood of art. The settings to these photographs, however, indicate these artists' actual and conceptual distance from the metropolitan bohemia.

In 1868 it was noted by the *Saturday Review* that the recently inaugurated oil exhibition at the Dudley Gallery had 'fallen under the kind patronage of the St John's Wood school' (*Saturday Review*, 26, p. 684). Two years later the *Art-Journal* wrote admiringly:

> The strength of the Dudley Gallery has been that it represents not one party, but many parties, that it asserts equal rights for all artists, whether recognised or unrecognised, simply on the basis of individual merit.
> *Art-Journal*, 9, p. 372

This philosophy greatly appealed to one artist who was 'unrecognised' in England. In the summer of 1868 Edouard Manet made a brief visit to London in order to explore the possibilities for the exhibition and sale of his paintings. On his return to France he wrote to Emile Zola:

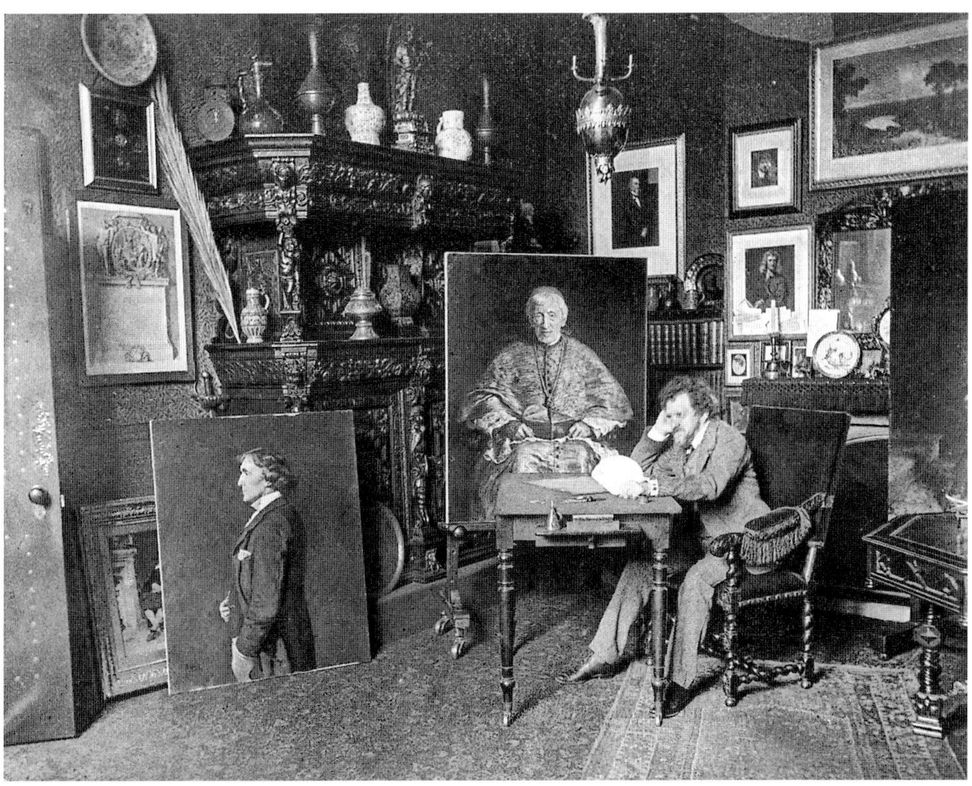

Fig. 13 Frank Dudman, *Thomas Oldham Barlow*, 1883, photogravure, 168 × 212mm, from J.P. Mayall, *Artists at Home*, 1884, National Portrait Gallery.
Wynfield's portrait of Barlow hangs above his head to the left of the landscape.

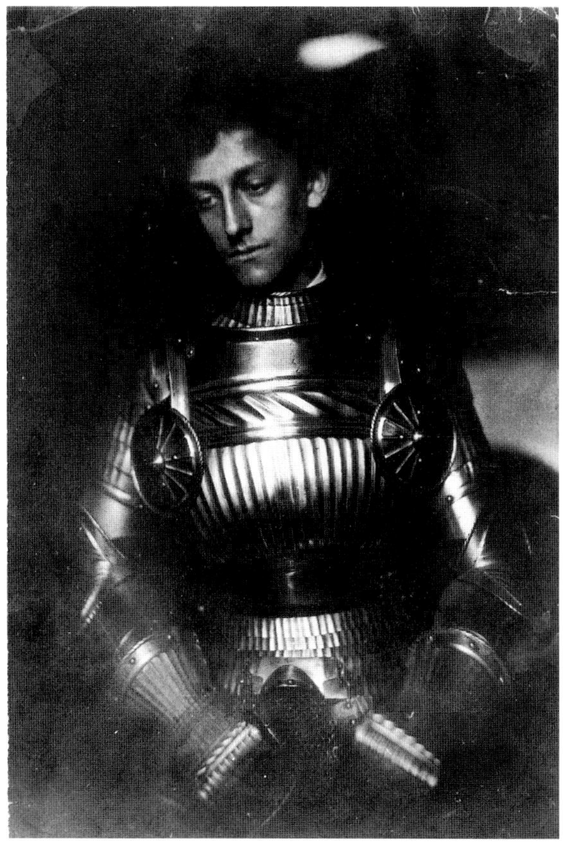

Fig. 14 Samuel Butler, *Johnston Forbes-Robertson in armour*, 1870, photograph, St John's College, Cambridge, Butler Collection.

> I went to London a few days ago and was delighted with the trip. I was very well received. I feel there is an opening for me over there, and I'm going to try it out next season. I saw some artists who were very kind and strongly recommended me to exhibit! They're not given to the kind of petty jealousy we have over here, most of them are real gentlemen ...

Although we know very little about Manet's time in London we can be certain that one of the 'real gentlemen' whom he came across was Wynfield because, in another letter written on his return, Manet noted his intention to write 'Mr Wynfield' a thank-you note. In Wynfield's portrait of Manet (pl. 37) the French artist wears contemporary dress. This is also true of the portrait that he made of Manet's friend and guide in London, Alphonse Legros (pl. 39). Like the American sculptor William Wetmore Story (pl. 38), neither Manet nor Legros could be claimed for the British school of art. Nonetheless, by subjecting them to his distinctive portrait treatment Wynfield could claim them as members of the artistic fraternity.

By the end of the 1860s the idea that all artists were brothers was coming under increasing stress. The artists of Wynfield's circle had made 'the Dudley', as it was commonly known, their own by making it the first gallery in London where it was possible to exhibit drawings and sketches in their own right. Storey's and Marks's memoirs, respectively titled *Sketches from Memory* and *Pen and Pencil Sketches*, relied upon an equation between the sketch and the youth of the artist. If the sketch symbolised the vitality of the young artist's untrammelled creativity then the finished painting symbolised the compromise of this youthful integrity in the pursuit of success. Beginning in the 1870s the bounty of middle-class patronage bought many of Wynfield's sitters the trappings of the respectable gentleman. We see the large studios of their suburban villas – more akin to the reception rooms of great houses than the sawdust-covered image of the *atelier* – in the series of photographs of *Artists at Home* issued by the Mayall studio in 1884. The portrait of Thomas Oldham Barlow from this series reveals that Wynfield's Rembrandtesque portrait of Barlow hung on his wall (fig. 13). Despite the fact that Barlow is surrounded by symbols of prosperity, he assumes a melancholic pose akin to that seen in Wynfield's portrait made twenty years earlier. Dudman's portrait is an eloquent testimony to George Leslie's claim that many successful artists of his generation were isolated by their wealth. The price of fame was an end to the bohemian camaraderie of youth.

Despite the fact that the Dudley Gallery offered an alternative exhibition venue for, amongst others, those artists who were rejected by the Royal Academy it was no *salon des refusés*. It was not until 1877 that London had a gallery that threatened the primacy of the Academy. In his memoirs Charles Hallé recalled that when Frederic Leighton heard that Sir Coutts Lindsay was planning to establish the Grosvenor Gallery he responded that such an endeavour would be 'unpatriotic' (*Notes*, p. 144). Although Hallé gave no explanation of this remark it would appear that Leighton saw through the oft-repeated claim that the gallery's policy of exhibition would not be biased towards those artists, such as Burne-Jones and Simeon Solomon (pl. 32), whose works had been rejected by the establishment. A year after the new gallery opened Leighton was elected president of the Royal Academy and knighted by the Queen. It was then that the artistic brethren of former days became polarised between the establishment and the avant-garde. During Leighton's presidency a number of Wynfield's closest friends found positions within what had become, according to Manet, the London art world's 'House of Lords'. William Frederick Yeames's decision to donate his collection of Wynfield photographs to the Royal Academy on his retirement from the position of librarian in 1911 was undoubtedly based upon the number of his sitters who had become members and associates. Ironically, amongst those who did not achieve such honours was Wynfield, the only member of the St John's Wood Clique not elected to the Royal Academy.

In the autobiographies and memoirs written by members of the Clique Wynfield is accorded significantly less space and less affection than the other members of the circle. It would appear to be more than coincidence that the authors of these volumes also demonstrate a wish to distance themselves from their penchant for posing as noblemen. Felix Moscheles stressed in his reminiscences of bohemia that the sketches that he and Du Maurier made of each other as '*bons princes*' were an example of youthful folly. In his memoirs, George Storey went so far as to repudiate the 'so-called "Historical Art" ' which he had practised as a young man. Writing in 1899, Storey claimed that historical genre painting was a species of 'theatrical make-up' whereas a painting by Velasquez was 'a true page of history' in which 'not only were the costumes correct, but the actual men of the time where there before me' (*Sketches*, pp. 249–50). Wynfield died before he could make a similar recantation and, as we shall see, at the time of this death he was uniquely identified with the theatricality of his portrait photographs.

As early as 1871 Tom Taylor demonstrated unease about Wynfield's use of costume for his photographic portraits. According to Taylor the costume lent 'something of the masquerade character' to what were otherwise 'one of the most valuable contributions to the Art-records of our times' (*D.W. Wynfield*, p. 86). We do not know whether by the time that Taylor wrote these words Wynfield had abandoned his practice of portrait photography. Although it is usually assumed that his photographic activities were limited to the first half of the 1860s this is unlikely to have been the case. His portrait of Manet almost certainly

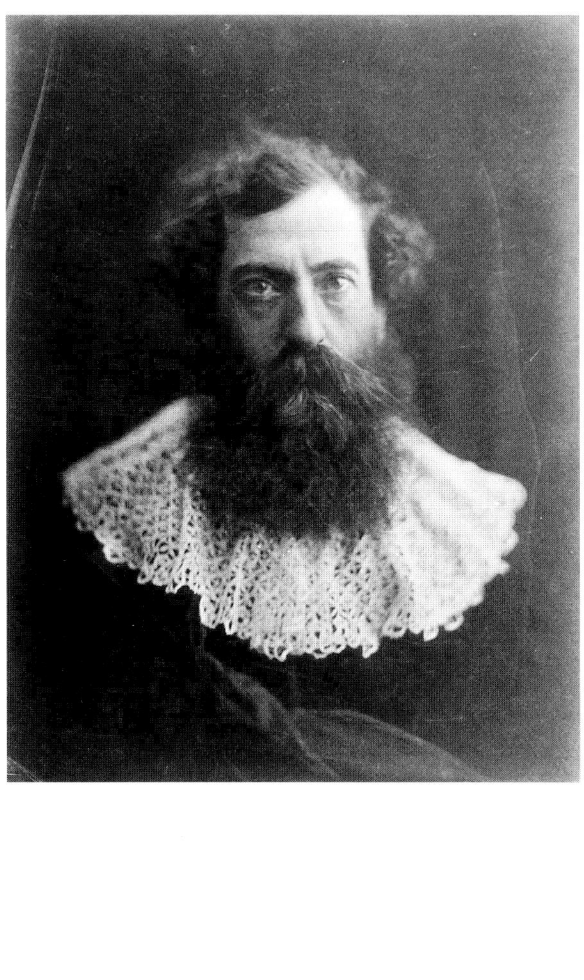

Fig. 15 J.M. Cameron, *Unidentified man*, 1866, albumen print, 351 × 275mm, National Museum of Photography, Film and Television, Bradford.

dates from 1868 and a comparison of his two portraits of Holman Hunt suggests that a significant lapse of time separated the sittings (pls. 28 and 29). The fact that Hunt does not wear historical costume in the later portrait suggests that Wynfield may have, at some stage, abandoned its use. He could not, however, escape an identification with the 'masquerade character' of his most typical portraits. At the time at which Wynfield's contemporaries were finding establishment success, the new rising generation saw their own aspirations mirrored in this style of photography. In 1870 Samuel Butler photographed the seventeen-year-old Johnston Forbes-Robertson according to 'Mr Wynfield's method' in the back room of Heatherley's (formerly Leigh's) wearing a suit of armour belonging to the school (fig. 14). A small number of costumed portraits by Wynfield have labels which identify them as having been issued by 'Heatherley's Studios' under John Crompton; Crompton's directorship of Heatherley's began in 1887, the year of Wynfield's death.

It would appear that it was not only Wynfield's photographs that became too closely identified with the preferences of youth. Marks's description in his memoirs of the involvement of the St John's Wood Clique and their friends with the Artists' Rifle Corps suggests that this was little more than a pose which enabled them to play-act as soldiers without ever seeing active duty. Wynfield, however, Marks implied, neglected his artistic duties for his military ones. The fact that Wynfield remained in the corps, eventually rising to the Captain of 'H' company in 1880, implies a persistent desire on his behalf for the homosociality of the all-male fraternity. We catch a glimpse of Wynfield in the guise of the military captain in the memoirs written by Colonel May. May remembered his surprise when, as a new recruit, he found himself confronted with a captain who sported a 'bushy beard and comfortable artistic costume' (*Memories*, pp. 19–20). Nevertheless, he soon developed a great attachment for the artist-soldier who asked his ensigns to treat him as a friend. The suggestion that Wynfield cultivated a paternal demeanour finds an intriguing parallel in the anecdote that it was Wynfield who gave the impoverished Fred Walker his first paintbox. But while Walker's premature death at the age of thirty-four was much lamented by his friends and contemporaries, his patron's early death at forty-nine was not.

One of the most striking features of Wynfield's photographic portraits is that, with the exception of the study of his sister (pl. 43), they are all of men and can hardly be a coincidence that the publication of *The Studio* came soon after the highly controversial admission of women to the Royal Academy schools. According to George Leslie, the admission of women put a stop to the boisterous, bohemian pranks that students had enjoyed there since the Academy's foundation. It also, so he claimed, had a deleterious effect on artistic standards. Nonetheless he conceded, as did Marks in his memoirs, that the invasion of the all-male enclave of the Royal Academy was inevitable and that it even had its benefits. Had Wynfield written his memoirs he may have come to a different conclusion. Wynfield was the only one of the original seven members of the Clique who did not marry; he died a bachelor. For the artists of this circle, marriage was a rite of passage in the transition from bohemian nonconformity to conformity; it was a guarantee of the essential moral purity that was required in order to maintain the Victorian bohemian as a gentleman. To remain unmarried was to no longer be able to elide the transgressive aspects of the bohemian existence with reference to the naivety of youth; it was a decision which cast the bachelor under suspicion of the wilful immorality of artists such as Simeon Solomon, arrested in 1873 for homosexual offences. In this light it is tempting to suggest that Wynfield's prolonged bachelorhood, and even the geniality which marked him as a 'real gentleman', became a source of anxiety for his friends.

In a letter in which G.F. Watts responded to one of Julia Margaret Cameron's many requests that he appraise her photographs, he told her that if she would only correct her technical 'shortcomings' she would be recognised as a great artist. He wrote:

> The jewel of perfection I speak of is best found because it exists in connection with extraordinary artistic qualities in some 3 or 4 of Winfield's [sic]: Val, Fred Walker & Oldham Barlow and one or two others. You should make an exchange with Winfield and keep these as tests of your own.

We do not know whether Cameron made the proposed exchange but we do know that she continued to be less interested in manipulation then artistic effect. The fact that there are only a handful of portraits by Cameron in which the sitter wears 'medieval' costume suggests that she did, however, listen to Watts's suggestion in another letter that he preferred her portraits in which the sitter did not wear ruffs (fig. 15). Cameron's photography quickly came to deviate from that of Wynfield's in other ways as well. Even before she increased the size of her plates Cameron would stress at every opportunity that her style of photography was completely original. At the very moment at which originality was set to become the defining criteria of artistic production Wynfield, on the other hand, produced a set of photographs that celebrated artistic heritage and influence. His discreet attempts at promoting his photographs, and in particular his decision to publish them anonymously, were at odds with Cameron's relentless campaign to generate publicity for herself and her works. Wynfield's evident distaste for self-promotion may suggest a temperament out of step with the times but it should be remembered that he could not afford to promote himself as a photographer. His reputation as a painter would have been irreparably damaged if he was thought to have used photography to make his compositions. As both a woman and an amateur, however, Cameron had nothing to lose.

It would appear that Wynfield intended his photographic portraits to contribute to a celebration of the 'comprehensive mind' of the artist as it was to be seen in his graphic productions. The photographic and non-photographic press, however, identified them as a response to commercial portrait photography and used them as ammunition in the symbolic battle between hierarchical culture and democratising progress. Wynfield's representation of the artist as courtier was not understood by those who were not artists and for those who were, the portraits became an uncomfortable example of youthful vanity. In the third quarter of the nineteenth century the increasing credibility of aesthetic partisanship served to identify painterly eclecticism as a concession to bourgeois values. The proponents of 'art for art's sake' characterised narrative art as insular, poorly executed and reliant on the sentiments generated by the subject rather than the formal qualities of the composition. The fact that the members of the St John's Wood Clique had found popular success as young men further singled them out as an example of artistic compromise. Despite the fact that Wynfield's photography bears almost no stylistic relation to his painting, it certainly suffered by association. The notion that all artists were brothers could not be sustained when Wynfield's generation had become heroes or villains in their own right.

The Plates

The Artist

David Wilkie Wynfield, né Winfield, was born in India in 1837. His father was James Stainback Winfield, a captain of the 47th Bengal Native Infantry, and his mother was Sophia May Burroughes, the niece and adopted daughter of the artist Sir David Wilkie. Wynfield's illustrious namesake was also his godfather. Captain Winfield retired from the army and the family returned to England in the early 1840s. He died when his son was still a small child.

We know from a letter which Wynfield wrote to Tom Taylor in 1871 that he was 'originally destined for the church' but that he discovered that he did not wish to be a priest. Wynfield entered Leigh's art school in 1856 and had his first painting accepted at the Royal Academy exhibition three years later. The paintings which he produced in the first half of the 1860s were usually set in medieval or Renaissance times and frequently dealt with the tragic consequences of love. In the late 1860s he began to alternate between solemn subjects such as his *Oliver Cromwell on the Night Before his Death* of 1867 (Victoria & Albert Museum) and more light-hearted ones such as *The Rich Widow,* set in the Jacobean period, of 1869. In 1871 Wynfield exhibited at the Royal Academy his most acclaimed work, *The Death of Buckingham*, which depicted the murdered body of the favourite of Charles I.

In 1859, the year of Wynfield's debut at the Royal Academy, the family home was at 2 Bristol Gardens, Maida Hill; the following year his address was listed as 3 Park Place Villas in Paddington. The change in the spelling of his surname which was made at about this time was probably owing to the need to distinguish himself from the established historical genre painter J.D. Wingfield. When, in 1867, all of his sisters had married and left home, Wynfield and his mother moved to a house a few doors away from his sister Annie and her husband William Frederick Yeames in Grove End Road, St John's Wood. Wynfield exhibited paintings at the Royal Academy nearly every year until his death from tuberculosis at the age of forty-nine. He is buried in Highgate Cemetery.

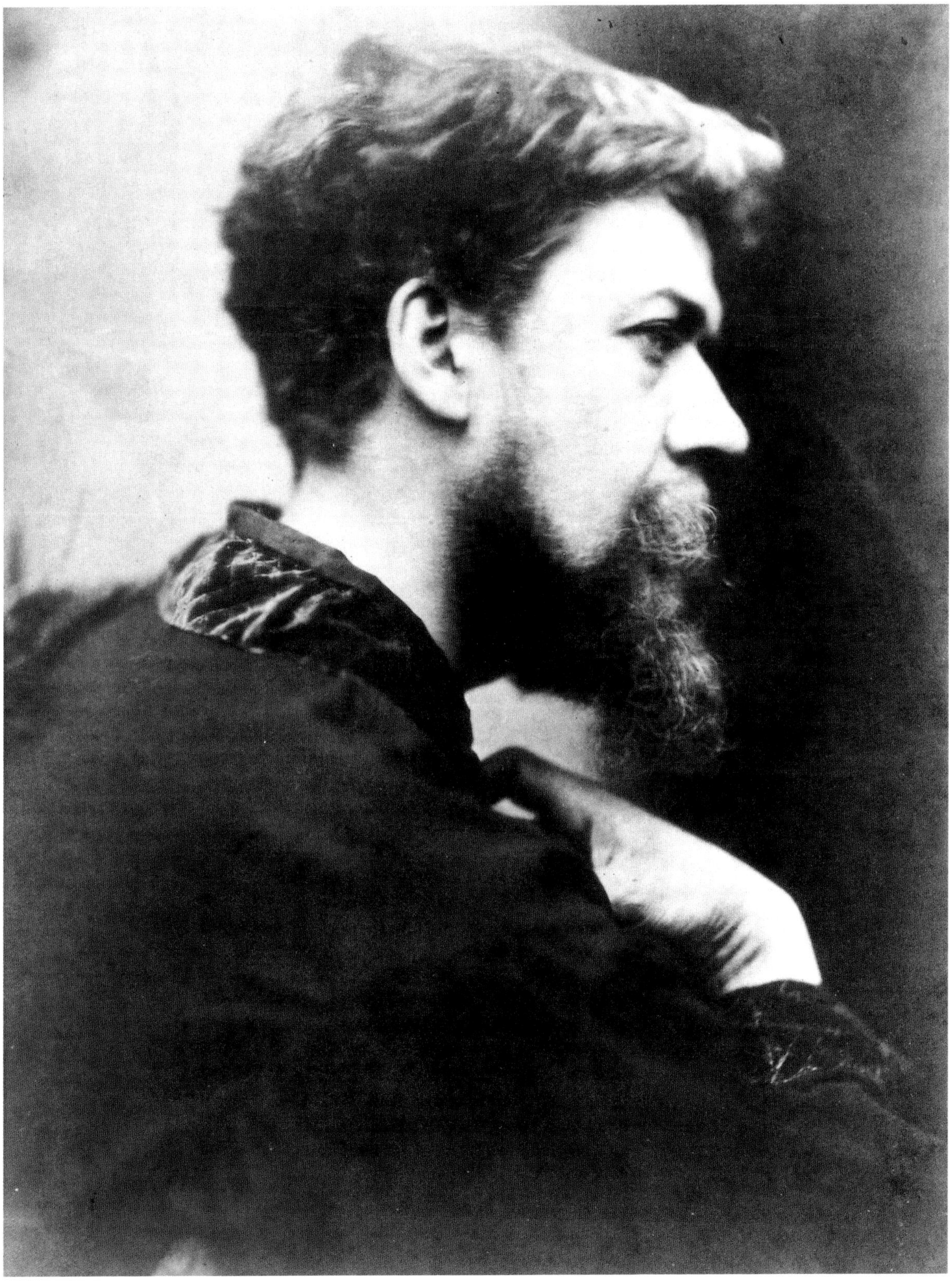

1 D.W. Wynfield, *Self-portrait, profile*, undated (1860s), albumen print, 218 × 169mm, Royal Academy of Arts.

The St John's Wood Clique

Five of the seven members of the St John's Wood Clique trained at the art school run by James Mathews Leigh at 79 Newman Street, the only school in London in the 1850s which was modelled on the *ateliers* of Paris. 'Dagger Leigh', said to be the model for Barker in *The Newcomes*, was known for his abrasive critiques of his students' efforts. It was however a mutual appreciation of these methods which drew the members of the clique together. They would meet once a week at each others' homes in the locale of St John's Wood, choose an episode from history, mythology or the Bible and give themselves a set time in which to each devise a composition. The symbol of the Clique, the gridiron, was a reference to their practice of 'grilling' one another over the success or otherwise of the results. The historical genre paintings which they exhibited at the Royal Academy and elsewhere were cabinet-sized works the subjects of which, as Tom Taylor put it, 'occupied the debateable ground between home-life and history'(*The Portfolio*, 12, 1870, p. 177).

The group portraits of the Clique which depict them in a medieval setting were taken at Hever Castle which in 1866 Yeames, Wynfield and Calderon hired for the summer and invited friends and their families to stay or visit. The presence of wives and children at Hever suggests that this was no bohemian enclave however. According to his niece, once married, Yeames was forbidden by his wife to paint from the nude. It is also said that Leslie advised Storey to remain within the '*chevalier* vein' in order to avoid painting *décolletée* women. It would appear that the Clique continued to paint in this vein after the majority of their contemporaries had abandoned it because of a wish to make an art that was acceptable to both women and children.

In middle age, former members of the Clique became part of the artistic establishment. Philip Hermogenes Calderon succeeded Frederick Richard Pickersgill to the keepership of the Royal Academy in 1887. George Storey became a lecturer in perspective and John Evan Hodgson was librarian and professor of painting from 1882 to 1895. Hodgson was succeeded as librarian by Yeames. It was on his retirement from the post of librarian in 1911 that Yeames donated his collection of Wynfield portraits to the Academy.

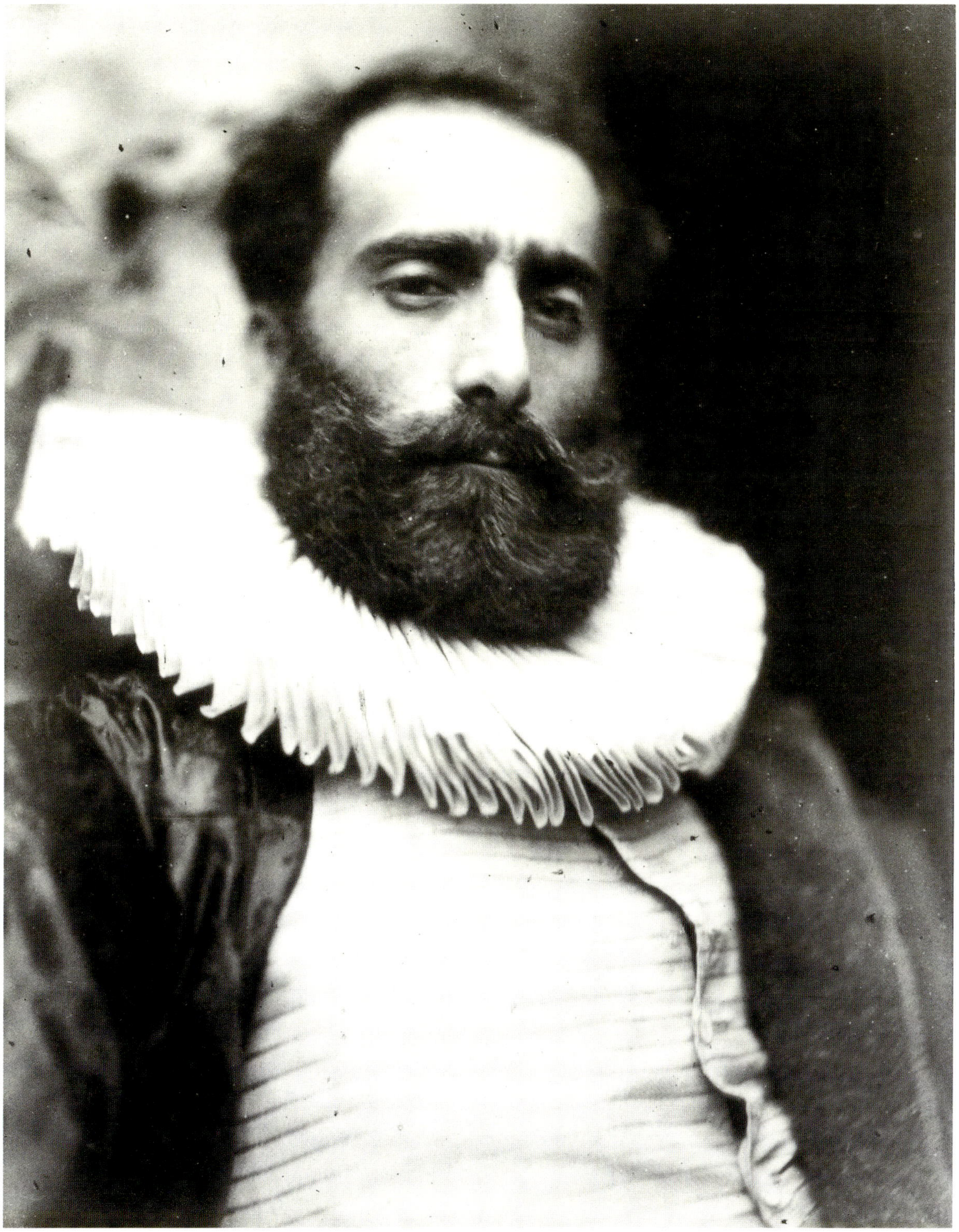

2 D.W. Wynfield, *Philip Hermogenes Calderon (1833–1898)*, undated (1860s), albumen print, 200 × 163mm, National Portrait Gallery.

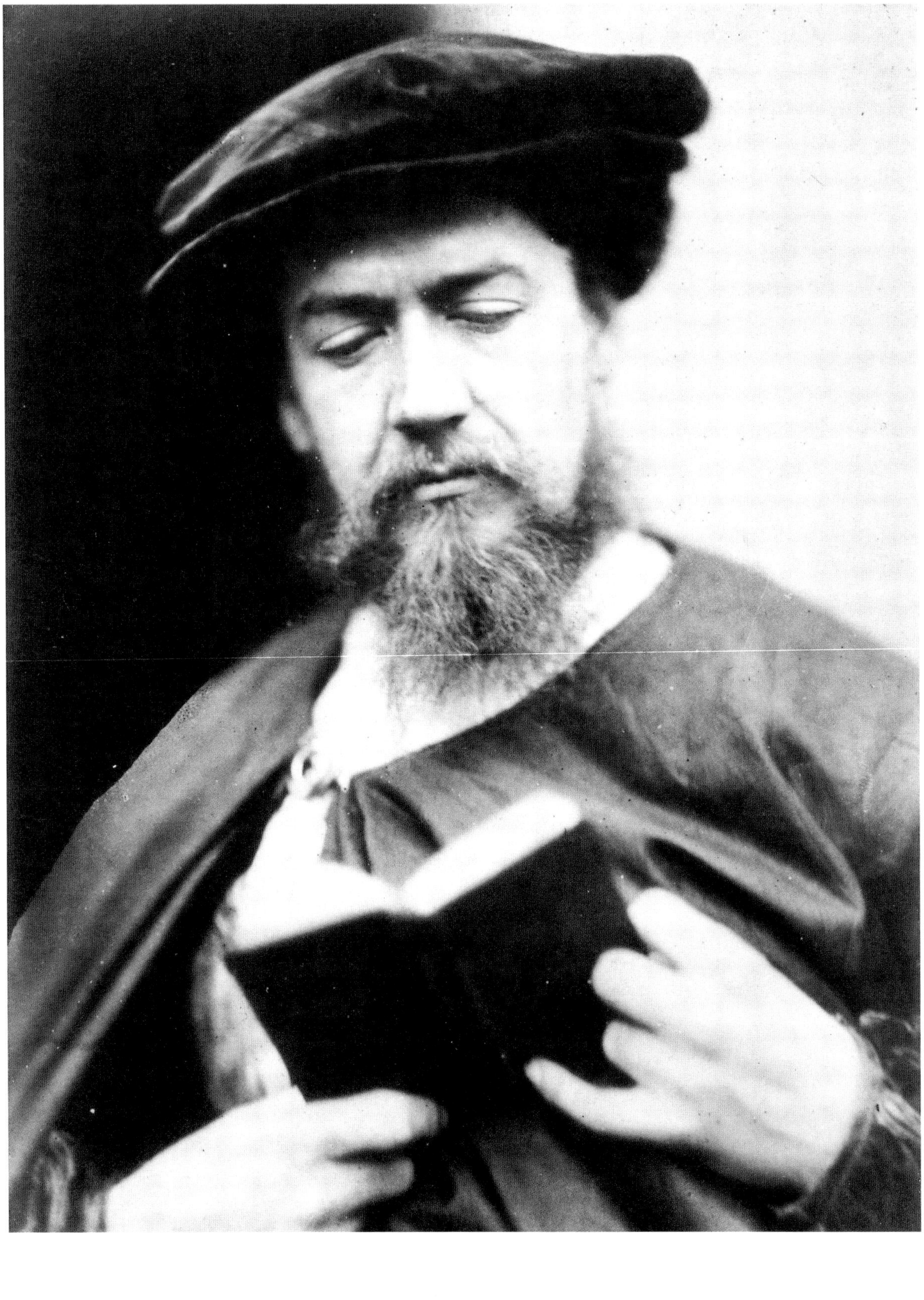

3 D.W. Wynfield, *Self-portrait, full face*, undated (1860s), albumen print, 212 × 161mm, National Portrait Gallery.

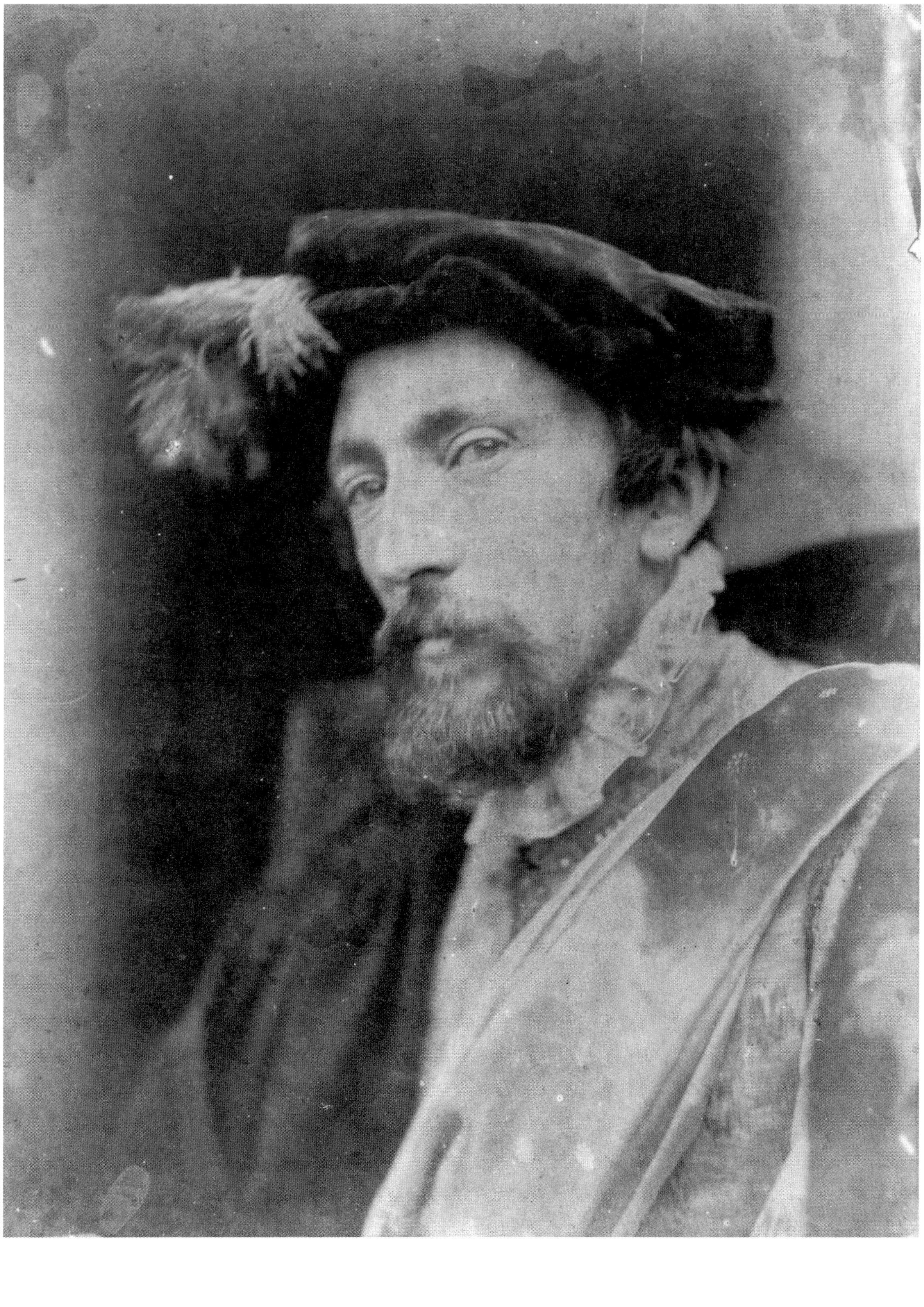

4 D.W. Wynfield, *John Evan Hodgson (1831–1895)*, undated (1860s), albumen print, 216 × 167mm, Royal Photographic Society.

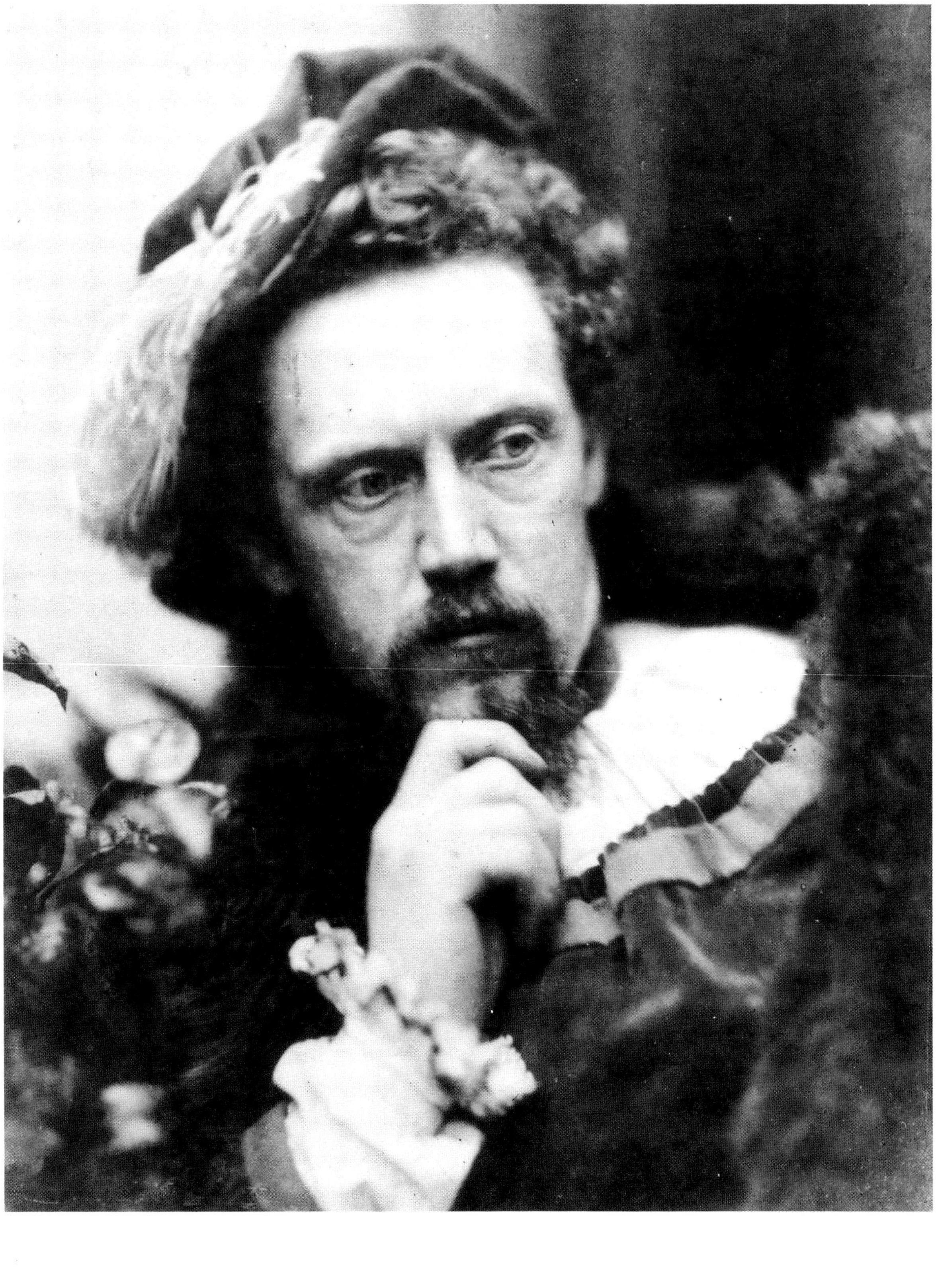

5 D.W.Wynfield, *Henry Stacey Marks (1829–1898)*, undated (1860s), albumen print, 199 × 161mm, National Portrait Gallery.

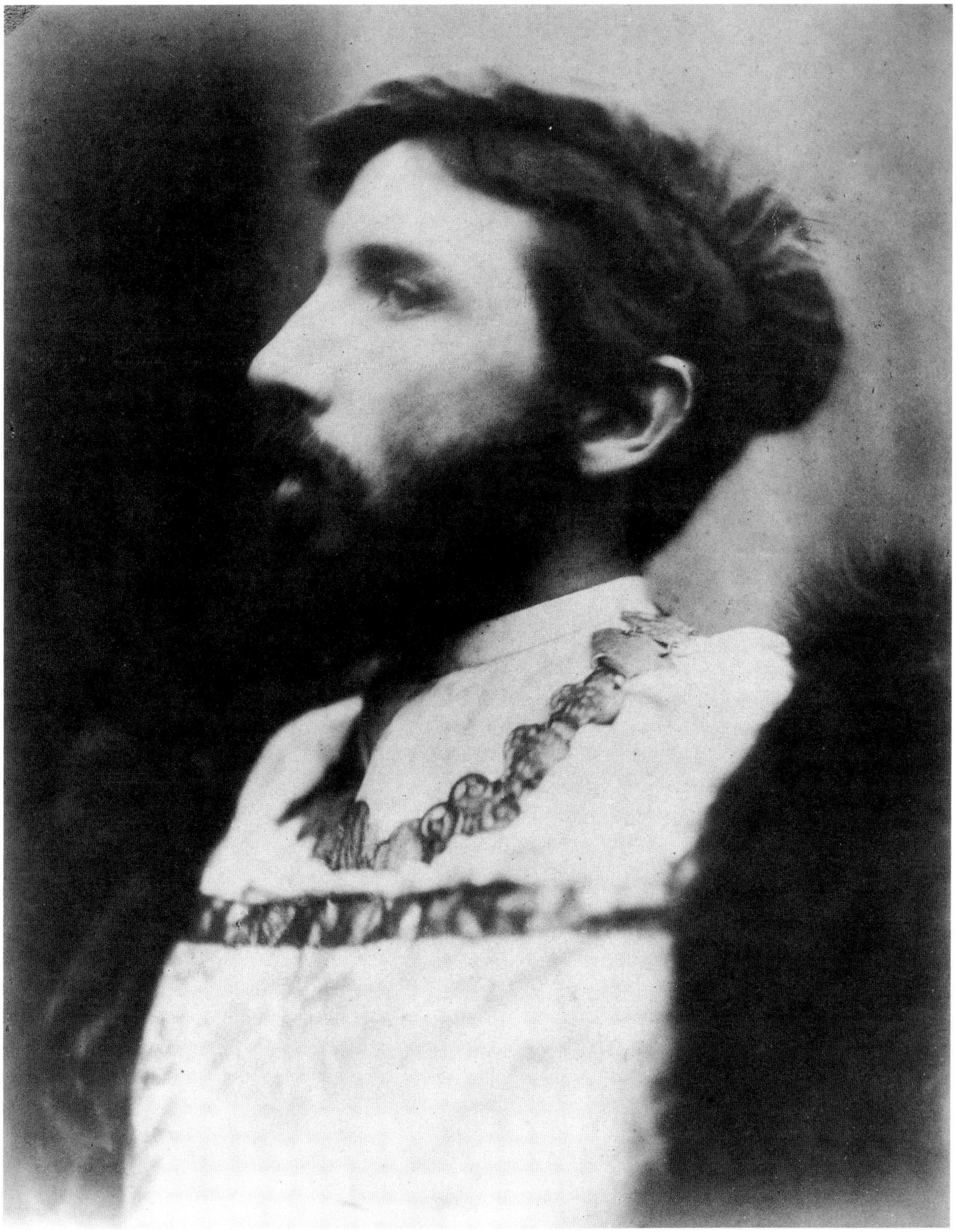

6 D.W. Wynfield, *George Dunlop Leslie (1835–1921)*, undated (1860s), albumen print, 210 × 164mm, Royal Academy of Arts.

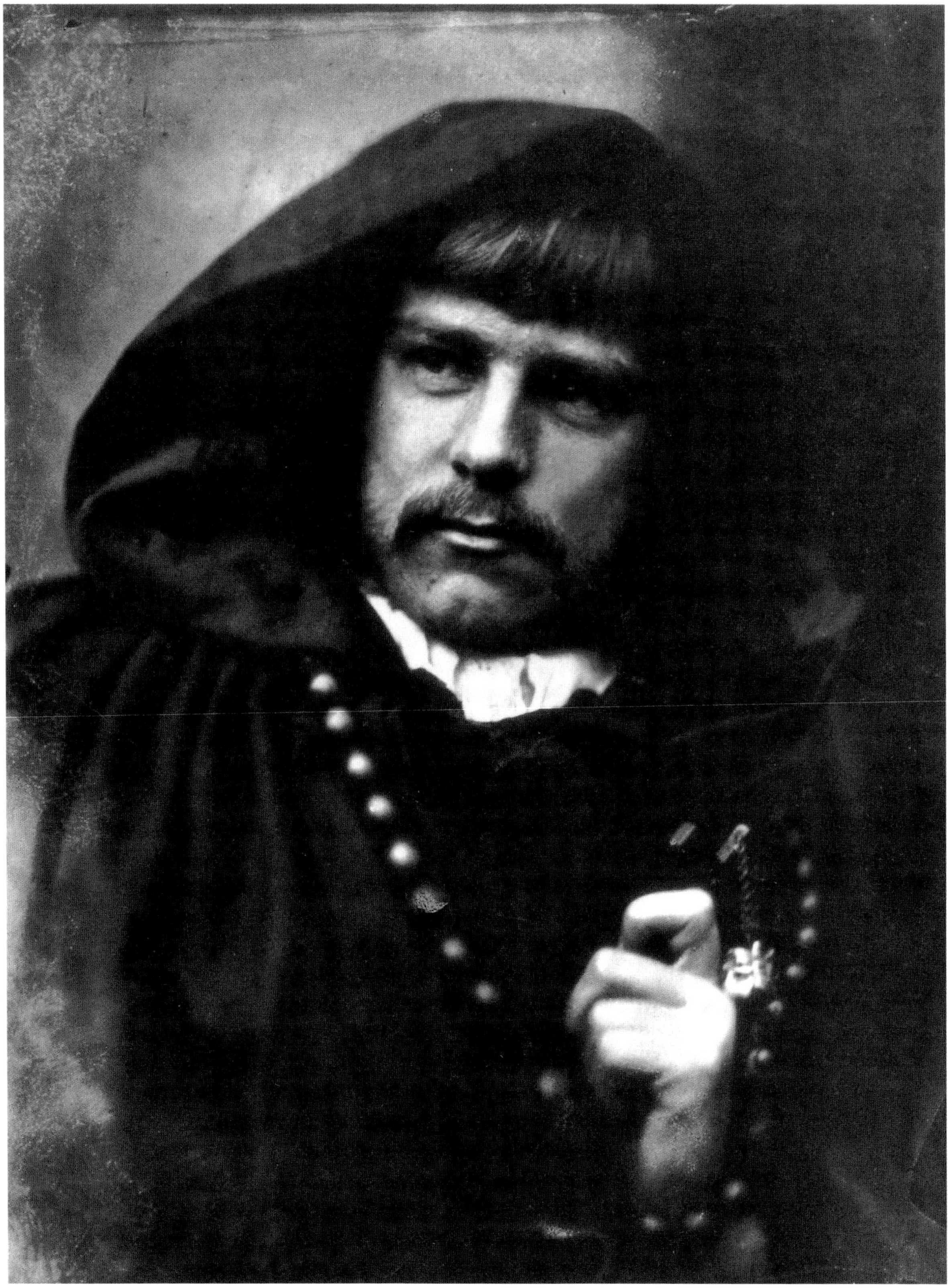

7 D.W. Wynfield, *George Adolphus Storey (1834–1919)*, undated (1860s), carbon print, 216 × 164mm, Royal Academy of Arts.

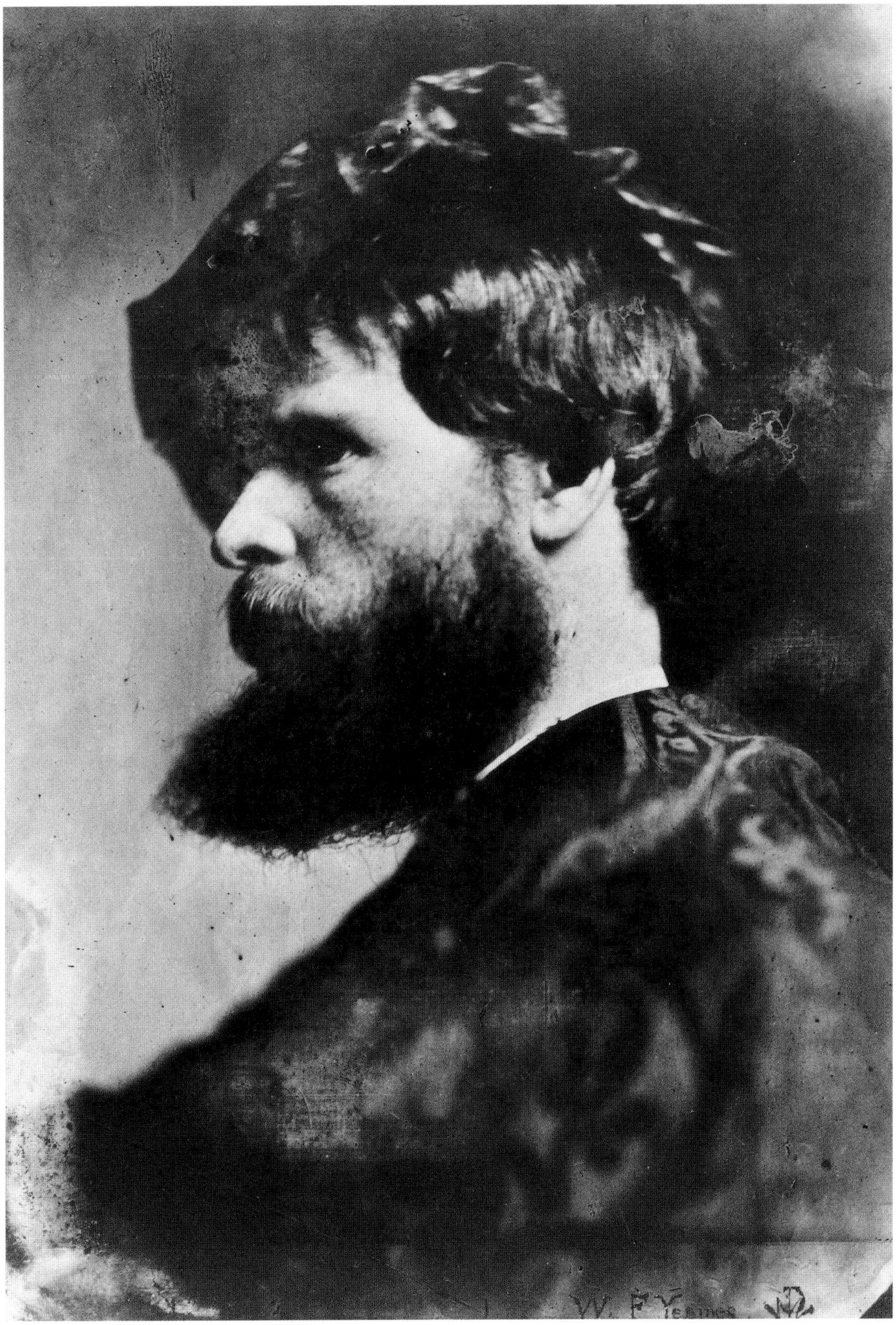

8 D.W. Wynfield, *William Frederick Yeames (1835–1918)*, undated (1860s), albumen print, 216 × 153mm, Royal Academy of Arts.

The Studio

In early 1864 Wynfield published a selection of his photographic portraits as *The Studio: A Collection of Photographic Portraits of Living Artists, Taken in the Style of the Old Masters, by An Amateur*. Each issue of *The Studio* cost a guinea and was comprised of four portrait photographs said to be 'in the style of' a continental school. We know that the fifth issue was in the style of the 'Flemish Schools' and included portraits of Thomas Oldham Barlow, William Gale, Myles Birket Foster and Charles Samuel Keene.

Described by George Leslie as 'a mezzotint engraver of considerable power' (*Inner Life*, p. 206), Thomas Oldham Barlow was renowned for his engraving of Millais's *A Huguenot* (Makins Collection), the picture which first brought the Pre-Raphaelite artist widespread popular acclaim. Wynfield's decision to photograph Barlow in the manner of a Rembrandt self-portrait is almost certainly a response to the contemporary revival of interest in Rembrandt's engravings.

William Gale was one of the many artists photographed by Wynfield who specialised in historical genre painting. The others include Robert Herdman, Eyre Crowe and Frederick Richard Pickersgill. The last two were honorary members of the St John's Wood Clique: Crowe was both a cousin of Thackeray and a cousin of the Prinsep family and Pickersgill was the son-in-law of Roger Fenton and an amateur photographer. He may have been influential therefore in Wynfield's decision to take up photography.

Part five of *The Studio* grouped together an engraver, a historical genre painter, a landscape painter and a graphic artist. By not seeking to distinguish his sitters according to the type of art in which they specialised, Wynfield provided a clue to the choice of title for the publication. In the market-place artists were divided by the need to compete with one another and to find their particular niche. In the studio, a male enclave even when part of a family home, artists could meet as equals and endeavour to recapture some of the bohemian camaraderie of their art-school days.

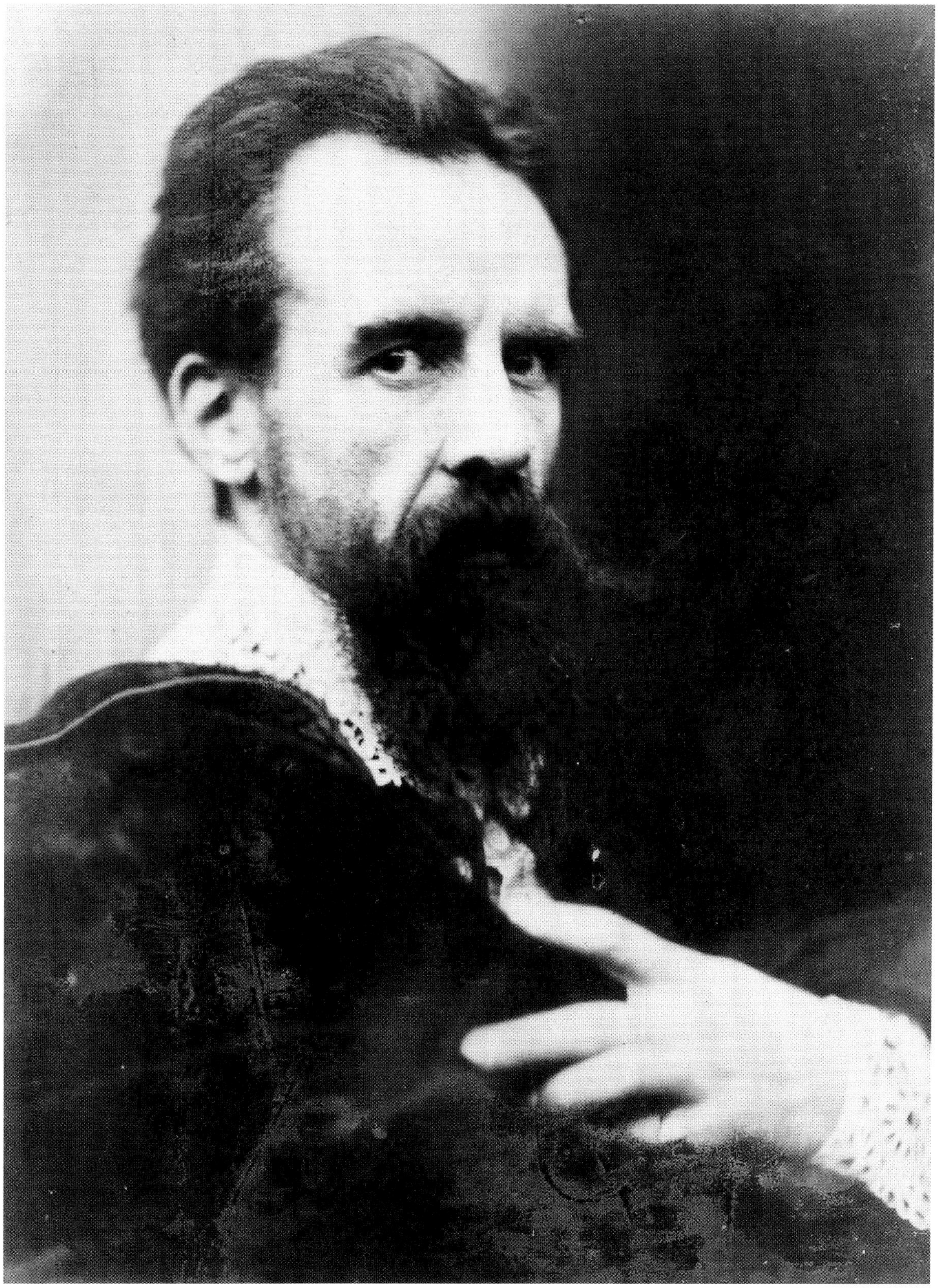

9 D.W. Wynfield, *William Gale (1823–1909)*, undated (1860s), albumen print, 212 × 161mm, National Portrait Gallery.

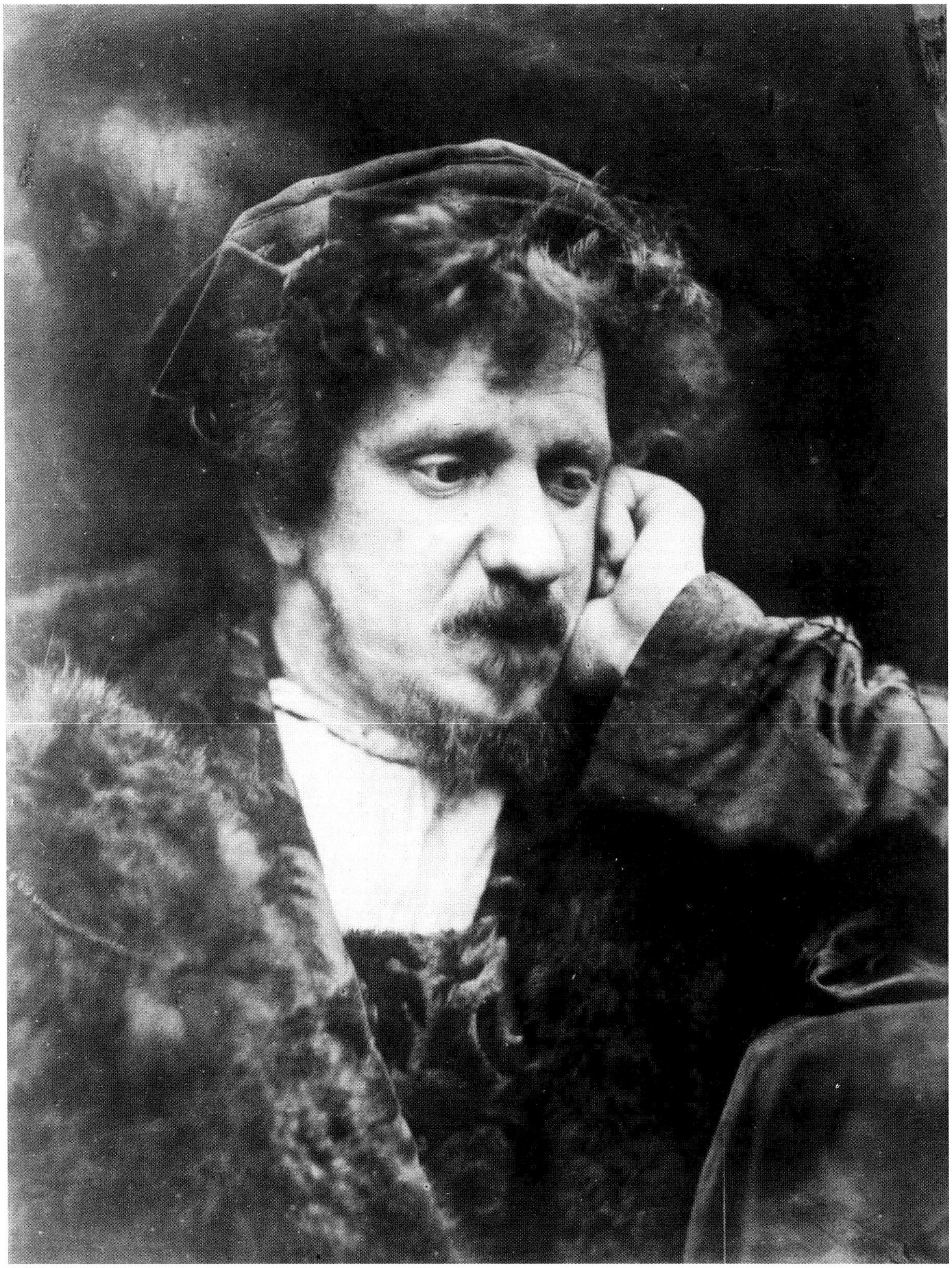

10 D.W. Wynfield, *Thomas Oldham Barlow (1824–1889)*, undated (1860s), albumen print, 208 × 162mm, National Portrait Gallery.

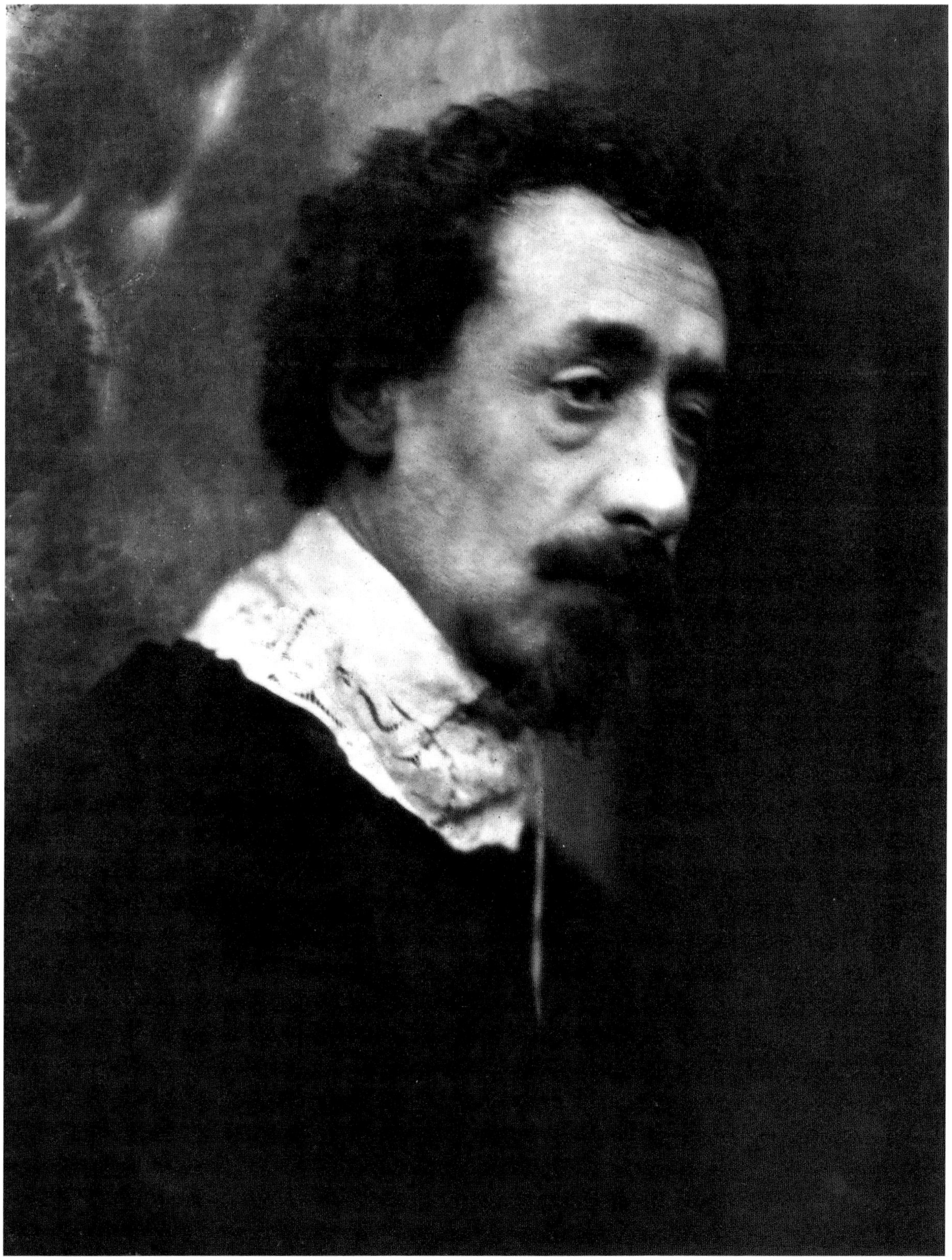

11 D.W. Wynfield, *Charles Samuel Keene (1823–1891), three-quarters profile*, undated (1860s), carbon print, 215 × 168mm, Royal Academy of Arts.

The Older Generation

A singular feature of the Victorian period was the vogue amongst artists for forming themselves into cliques and coteries. The first such grouping was The Clique, a sketching club comprised of Richard Dadd, Henry O'Neil, William Powell Frith and John Phillip. John 'Spanish' Phillip was elected A.R.A in 1857 and a full associate two years later. He earnt his nickname from his predilection for subjects taken from Spanish life. The painting which Phillip exhibited at the Royal Academy in 1865, *The Early Career of Murillo, 1634*, was typical of the self-referentiality of the art of this period. Wynfield's portrait of Phillip is another example of this practice: it is strongly reminiscent of William Dobson's oil portrait of Sir Edward Nicholas of c. 1645 (National Portrait Gallery). Phillip and Richard Ansdell travelled together to Spain in 1856 and later collaborated on a number of Spanish scenes. Ansdell, who had moved to London from Liverpool in 1847, was a successful artist known for his equestrian and sporting pictures.

A number of Wynfield's elder contemporaries had been involved in the proposed decoration of the new Houses of Parliament in the 1840s and 1850s, the scheme which many believed would revive history painting in Britain. In this moment of optimism William Dyce, John Rogers Herbert and Edward Armitage formed a coterie dedicated to the reinvigoration of historical art. Armitage was a pupil and admirer of Paul Delaroche, the French painter credited with the invention of the *genre historique*. Having worked on Delaroche's famous *Hemisphere of the Arts* in Paris, Armitage endeavoured to gain commissions in England for so-called 'monumental' art, mural decorative schemes for public buildings.

Alfred Elmore, like Armitage, spent many years in Paris before settling in London. Elmore's exhibited works were almost all of subjects from English, French or Italian history. He is however better known for his modern-life painting *On the Brink* of 1865 (Fitzwilliam Museum, Cambridge) in which a fashionably dressed young woman slumps outside a gambling den in the German resort of Homburg. Amongst the younger generation of painters of contemporary life, Wynfield photographed James Hayllar and Charles Perugini.

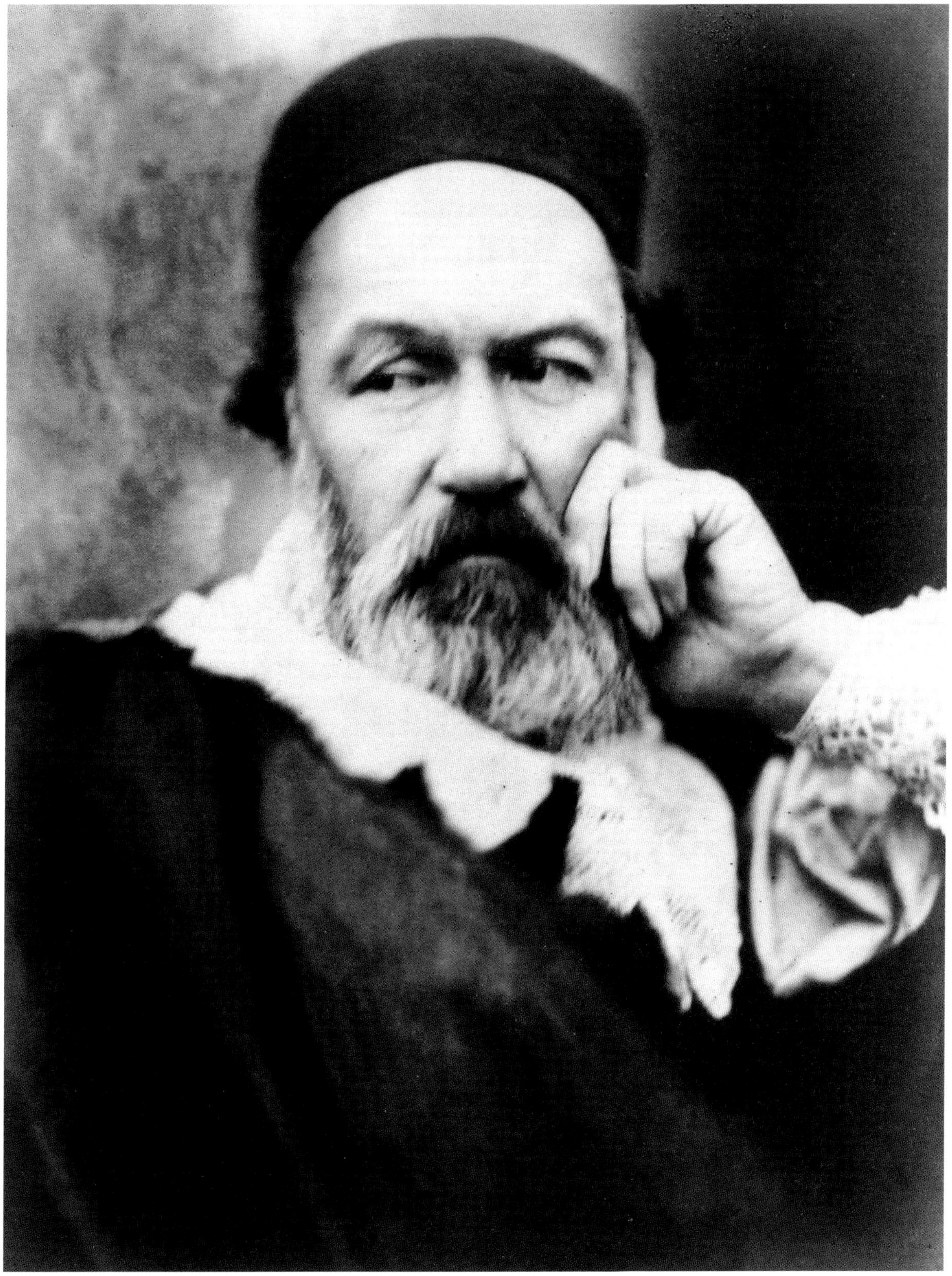

12 D.W. Wynfield, *Alfred Elmore (1815–1881)*, undated (1860s), albumen print, 211 × 161mm, Royal Academy.

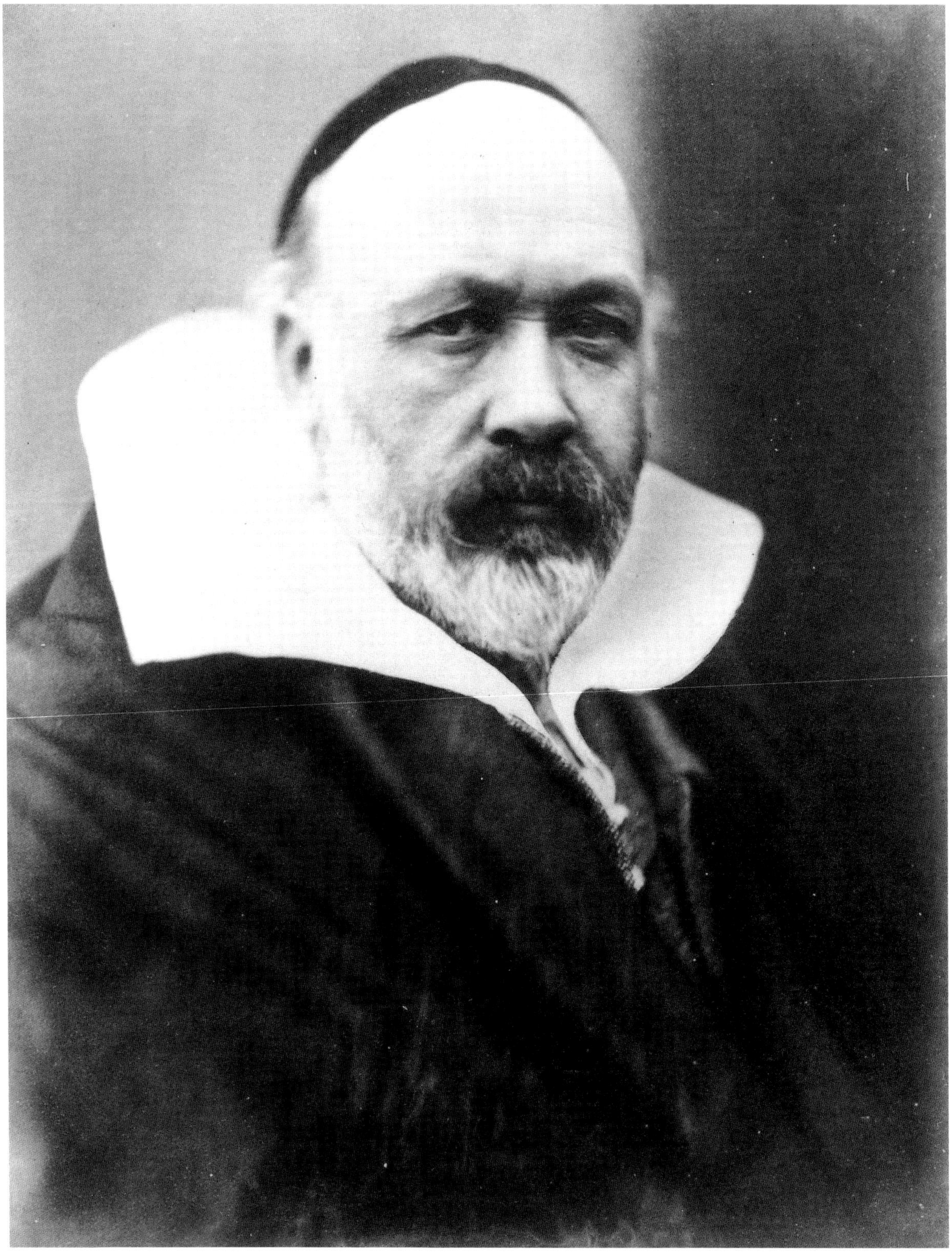

13 D.W. Wynfield, *John Phillip (1817–1867)*, undated (1860s), albumen print, 209 × 162mm, National Portrait Gallery.

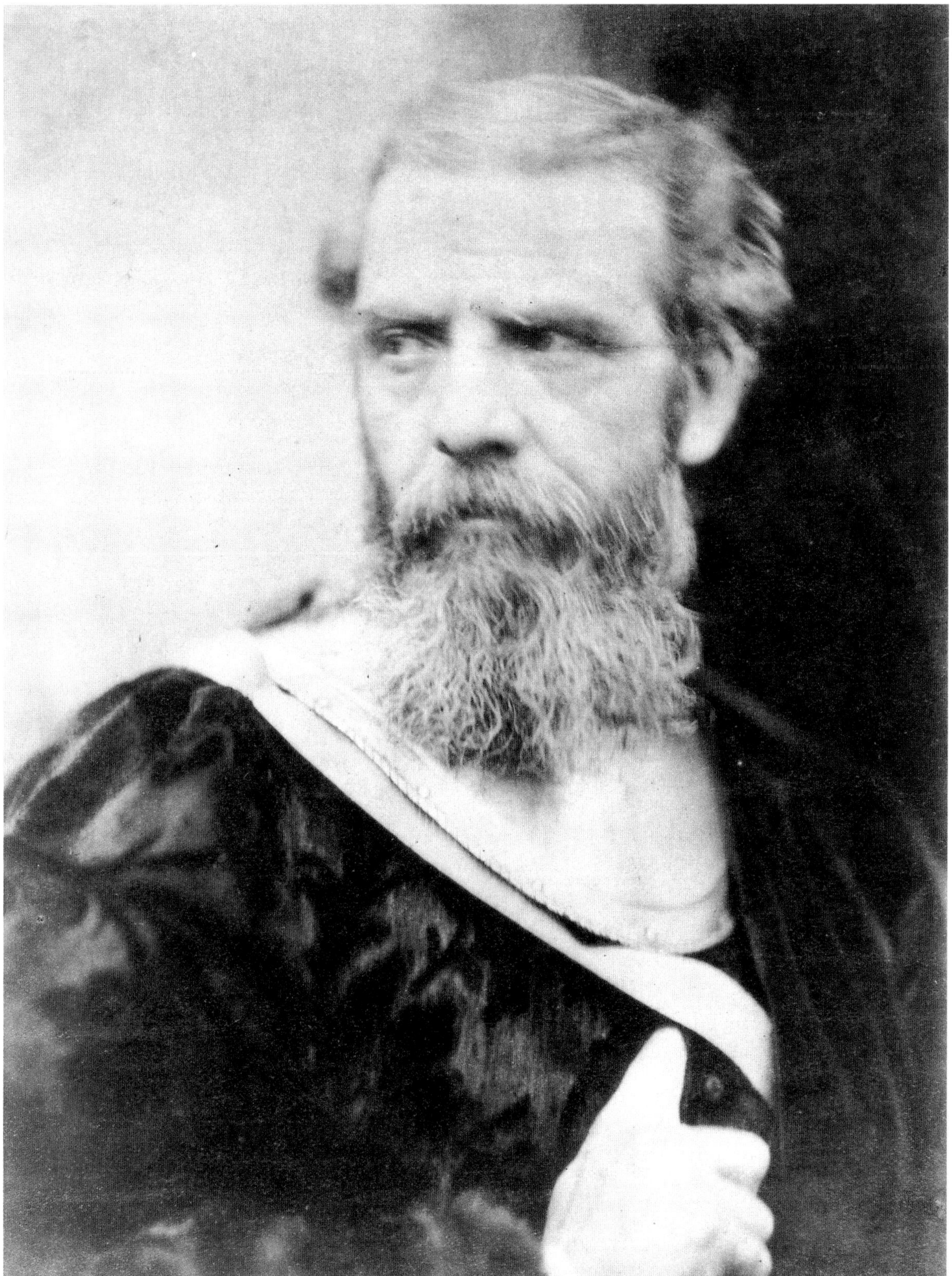

14 D.W. Wynfield, *Richard Ansdell (1815–1885)*, undated (1860s), albumen print, 212 × 161mm, National Portrait Gallery.

Architects

A number of Wynfield's portraits have a photographic facsmile of the sitter's signature preserved on the mount. The portraits which have these signatures tend to be of sitters who are immediately recognisable; for those sitters whose faces are less well known we have to rely upon a list which has been preserved with the collection of Wynfield's photographs donated by William Frederick Yeames to the Royal Academy. This list is likely to have been written some time after the portraits entered the collection and is not altogether reliable.

On this list the portrait of the man contemplating a flower is identified simply as 'Architect (Barber)'. The sitter is most likely to be William Swinden Barber who travelled in Italy with his fellow architect Frederick Pepys Cockerell, also photographed by Wynfield, for six months in 1855–6. If the sitter is Barber then it is the only known portrait of him in a public collection. The same is true of Wynfield's portraits of the architects Frederick Mew and Anthony Salvin Jr. The sitter identified on the Royal Academy list as a 'Railway Porter' bears more than a passing resemblance to George Edmund Street, the architect of the Royal Courts of Justice.

Wynfield's generation believed that in the Middle Ages there had been no hierarchical distinction drawn between the fine and the decorative arts. This was an immensely attractive idea for painters and architects who could only sustain the production of major individual works by collaborating on various decorative projects. In this light, it is surprising that there is no (known) portrait by Wynfield of William Burges, the man who inspired many of Wynfield's generation with his enthusiasm for the decorative arts of the Middle Ages. There is a photograph in the collection of the National Portrait Gallery of Burges in which he wears a medieval jester's costume but the portrait is in a different manner to that of Wynfield. Also in the collection is a fine drawing of 1858 by Jacques-Emile-Edouard Brandon of William Eden Nesfield, the architect cousin of Anthony Salvin Jr, wearing a medieval velvet cap and inscribed with the sitter's name and dates in medieval French.

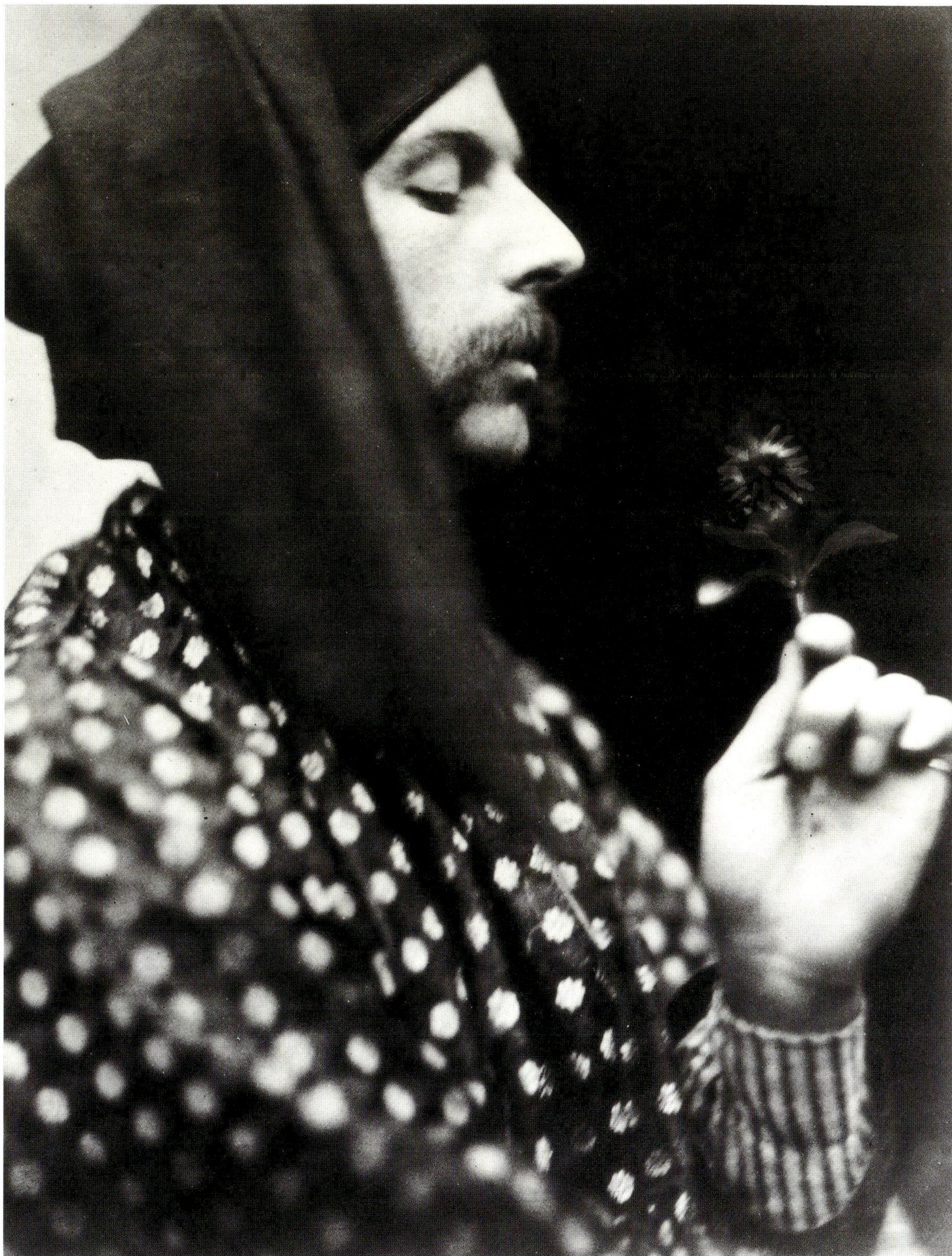

15 D.W. Wynfield, *William Swinden Barber* (fl.*1855–1898)*, undated (1860s), albumen print, 209 × 166mm, Royal Academy of Arts.

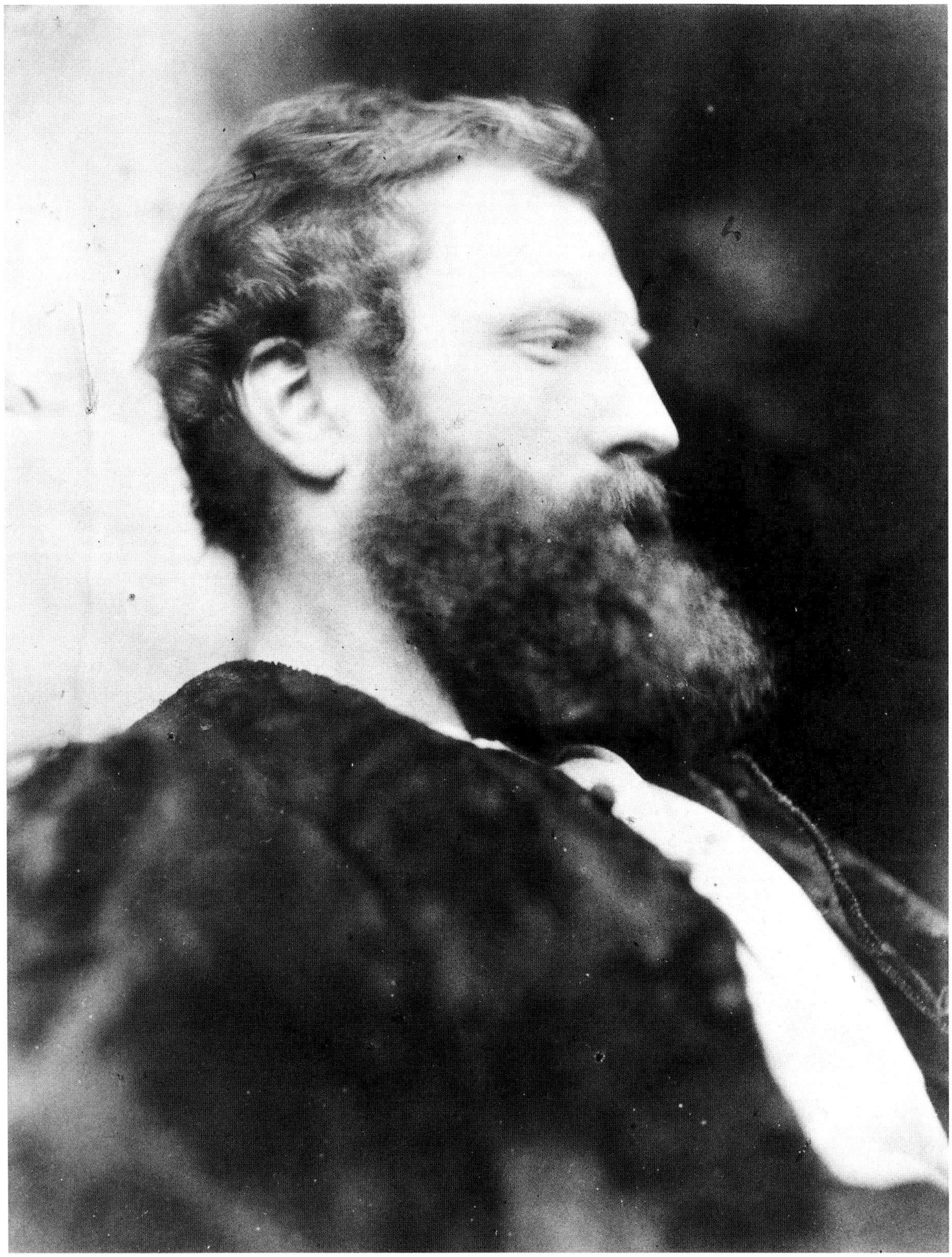

16 D.W. Wynfield, *Unidentified man, possibly George Edmund Street (1824–1881)*, undated (1860s), albumen print, 213 × 163mm, Royal Academy of Arts.

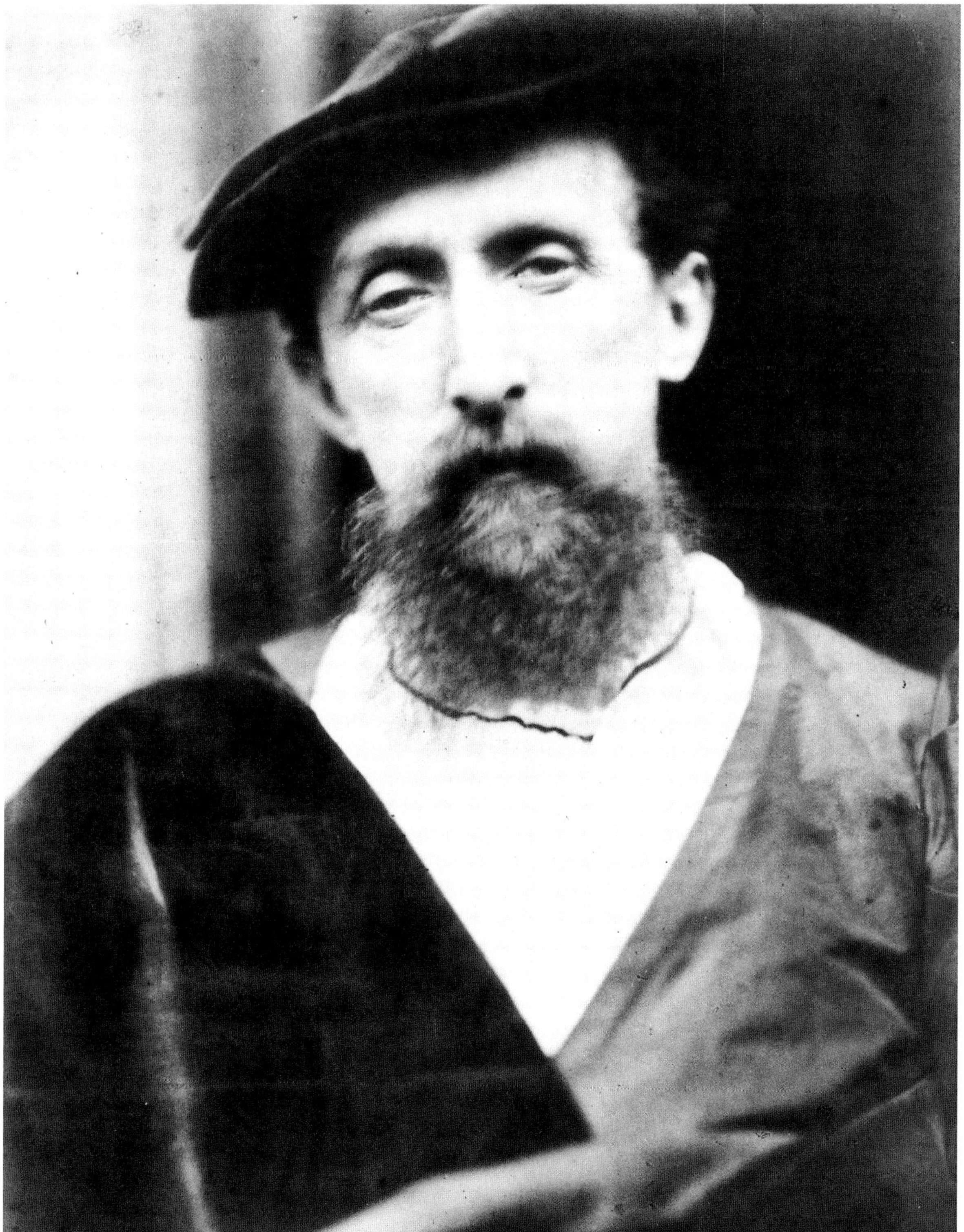

17 D.W. Wynfield, *Anthony Salvin Jr. (1827–1881)*, undated (1860s), albumen print, 205 × 163mm, Royal Academy of Arts.

Landscape and Genre Painters

Wynfield's portrait of Robert Taylor Pritchett, a now little-known painter of landscape and rustic scenes, is the only one of his photographs which is dated. The Latin inscription which appears in the top right corner of the portrait is likely to have been painted on the negative. It tells us that the photograph was made in London in 1864 when the sitter was thirty-six.

In the late 1850s the Dalziel brothers commissioned Myles Birket Foster to make a series of fifty full-page drawings to be published under the title *Pictures of the British Landscape*. This was eventually published in a reduced form by Routledge & Co with poems supplied by Tom Taylor. This was an immensely significant moment for the arts in Britain because the poems were a response to the art instead of vice versa. In 1861 Du Maurier had written to his mother that while at the offices of *Once a Week* he 'had the cheek to say that it bored me to illustrate other men's poems, and that I could draw quite well enough if I chose, to have poems written to my illustrations' (*Letters*, p. 29).

Thomas Faed was an immensely successful painter of scenes of Scottish peasant life. His most well-known work is *The Mitherless Bairn* which depicts a pitiful orphan being studied by the inhabitants of a humble cottage. Another painter of rustic scenes photographed by Wynfield found his means to be almost equal to the peasants that he depicted. As a young man George Heming Mason had been compelled by his father to train as a surgeon. After five years of study he rebelled and left England for Rome. Despite having almost no money on which to live he managed to teach himself to paint and later became known for his skilful depictions of rural life.

Wynfield also photographed Charles Thornely, the painter of river and coastal scenes, and George Price Boyce, the landscape painter in watercolour and collector of contemporary art better known for his diaries which, like Du Maurier's letters, are an invaluable source for picturing this generation in their private aspect.

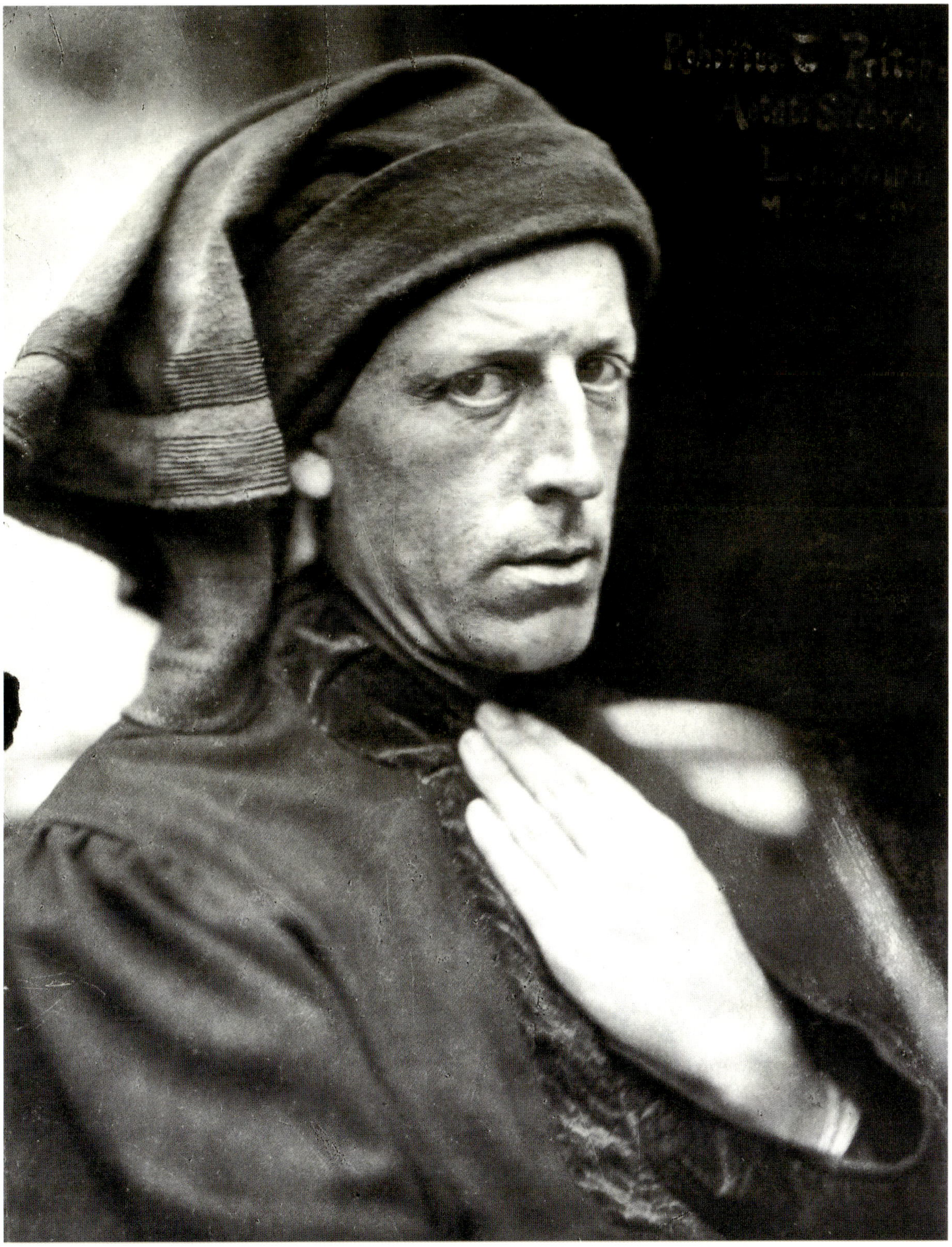

18 D.W. Wynfield, *Robert Taylor Pritchett (1828–1907)*, 1864, carbon print, 210 × 161mm, Royal Academy of Arts.

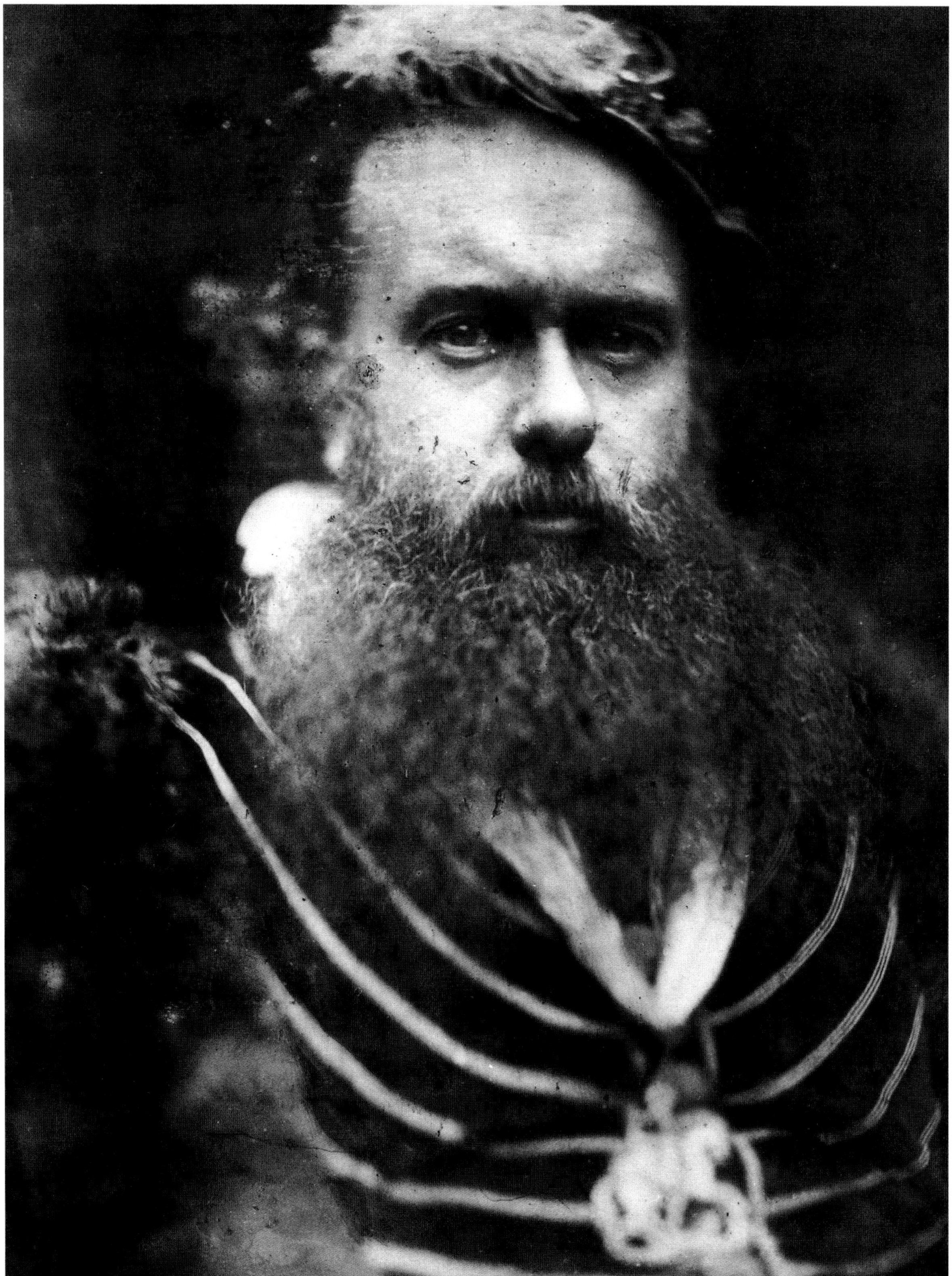

19 D.W. Wynfield, *Myles Birket Foster (1825–1899)*, undated (1860s), albumen print, 212 × 162mm, National Portrait Gallery.

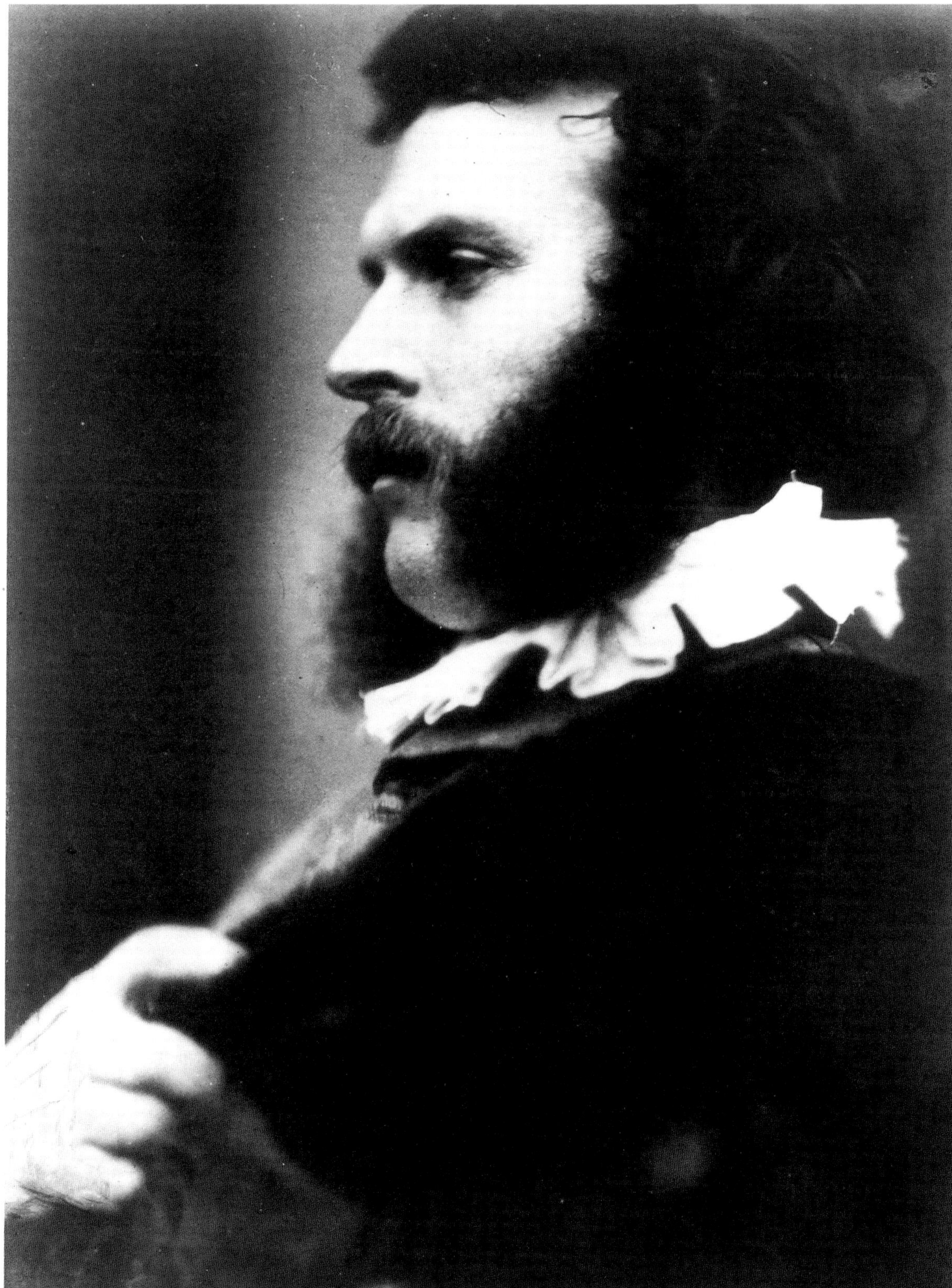

20 D.W. Wynfield, *Thomas Faed (1826–1900)*, undated (1860s), albumen print, 208 × 162mm, National Portrait Gallery.

Portrait Painters

Carl Haag was to be the only genuine court painter amongst Wynfield's sitters. Originally from Bavaria, in 1847 he moved to England where he was patronised by Queen Victoria and the Prince Consort; he was later appointed as painter to the Duke of Saxe-Coburg. Henry Tanworth Wells was also favoured by the British royal family. Even with their patronage, however, he could not sustain himself as a painter of miniatures because of the deleterious effect of photography on the market for such portraits. Instead of becoming a photographer as many of his contemporaries did, Wells turned to portraiture in oils. He was married to the artist Joanna Boyce, the sister of George, and lived on Campden Hill close to Arthur Lewis.

In August 1862 Field Talfourd wrote in his journal that 'Photography has nearly deprived me of work in my crayon drawings — I am studying with [Edward] Sterling in oil to the end of changing my style'. Talfourd is now best known for the chalk portrait of Elizabeth Barrett Browning (National Portrait Gallery) which he made in Rome in 1859 and which Robert Browning identified as the best likeness of her. In 1861 Talfourd found himself in competition with Joseph Middleton Jopling who, like his rival, spent that winter making portraits among the expatriate community in Rome. Jopling was a self-taught artist and a close friend of Millais; he later married the artist Louise Goode.

It is said that it was Edward Sterling who originally proposed the idea of an Artists' Rifle Corps. A series of discussion meetings were held in the studio of Henry Wyndam Phillips and he became the first Captain. Haag, Jopling and Talfourd were also founding members. Jopling was later commissioned to make drawings of the Queen inspecting the troops and Wells' first major work in oils was of Lord Ranelagh in his uniform as Colonel of the South Middlesex Rifle Corps. In 1866 Wells exhibited *Volunteers at a Firing-Point* (Royal Academy, London) to critical acclaim.

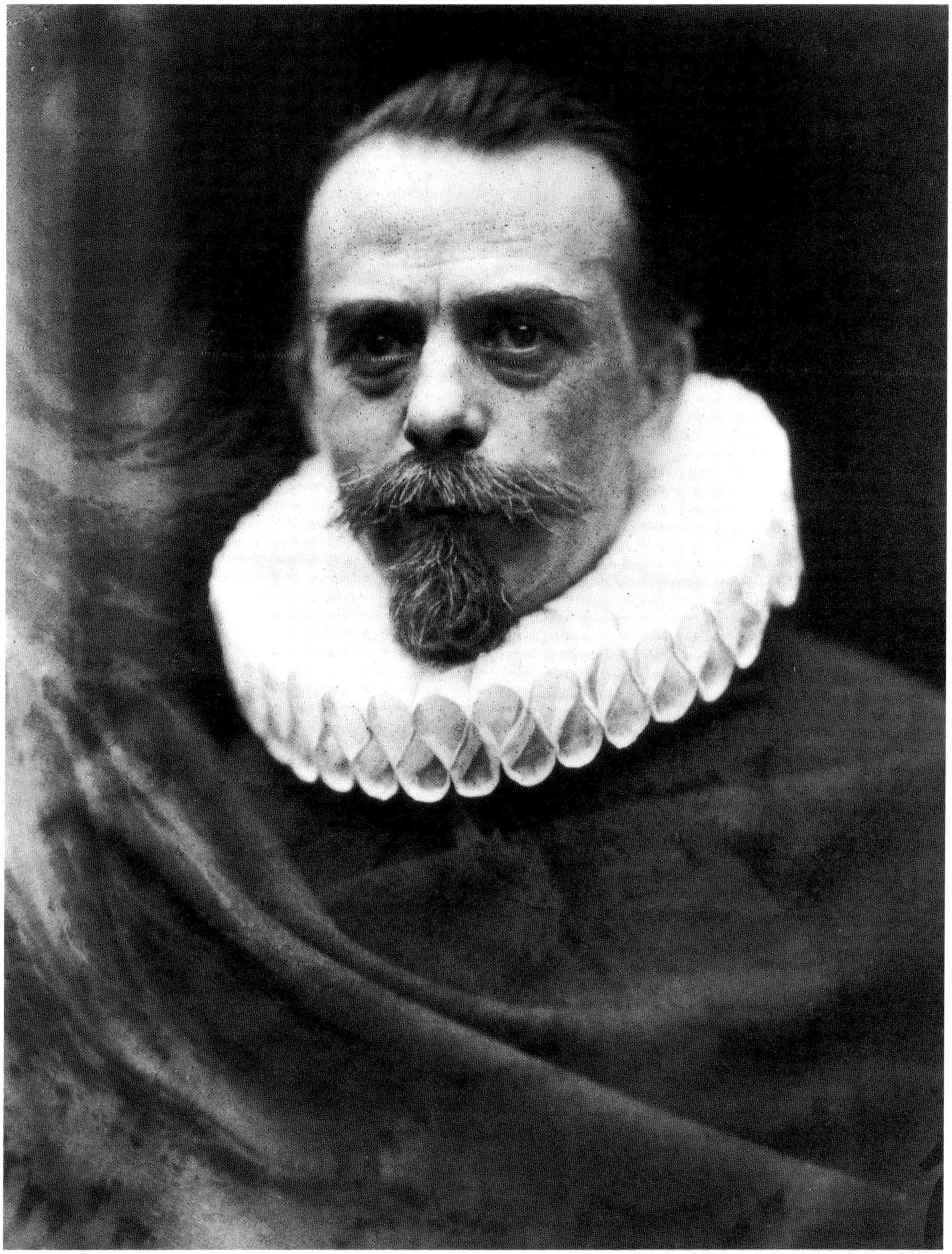

21 D.W. Wynfield, *Carl Haag (1820–1915)*, undated (1860s), albumen print, 209 × 164mm, Royal Academy of Arts.

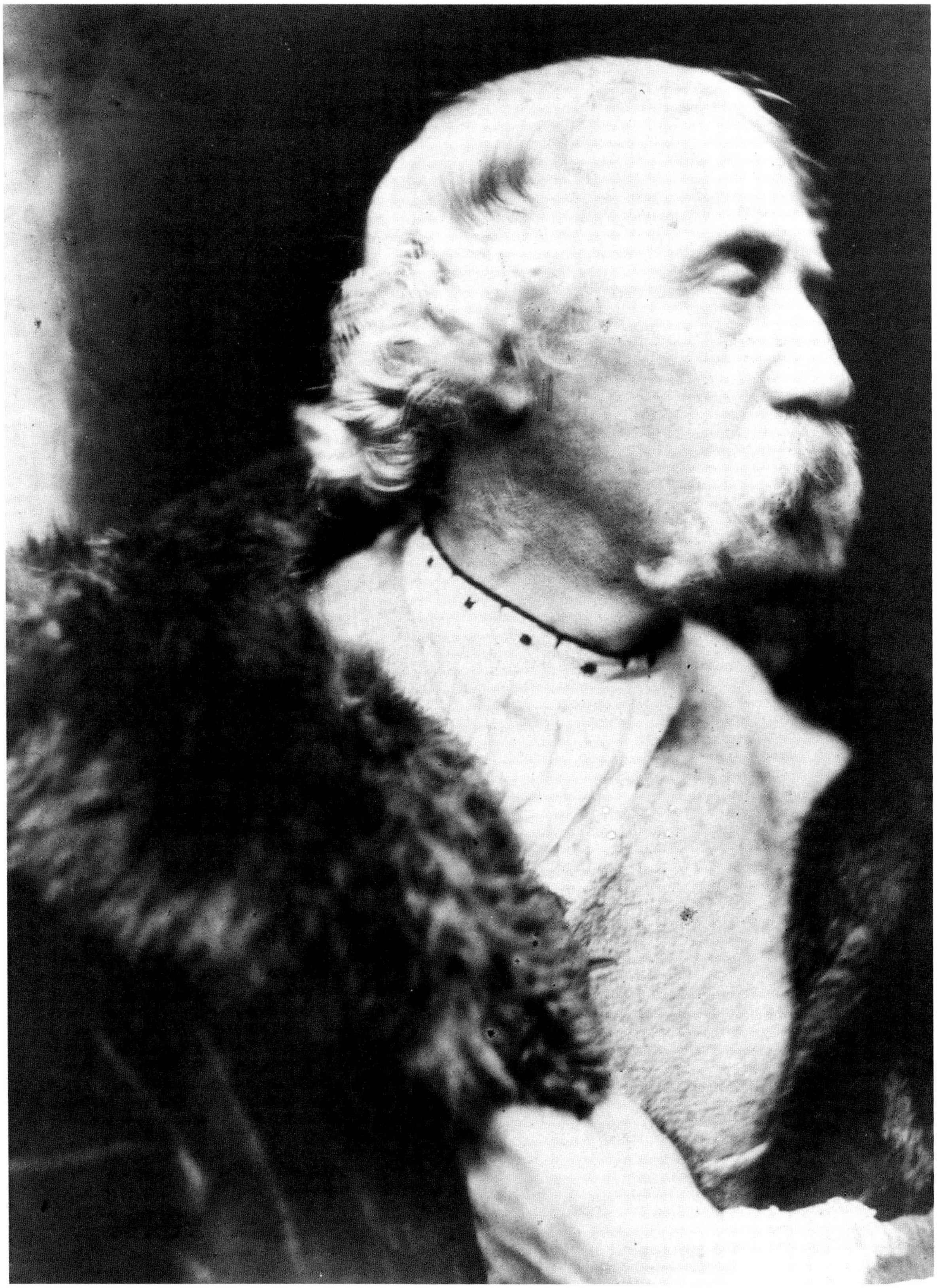

22 D.W. Wynfield, *Field Talfourd (1814–1874)*, undated (1860s), albumen print, 215 × 163mm, Royal Academy of Arts.

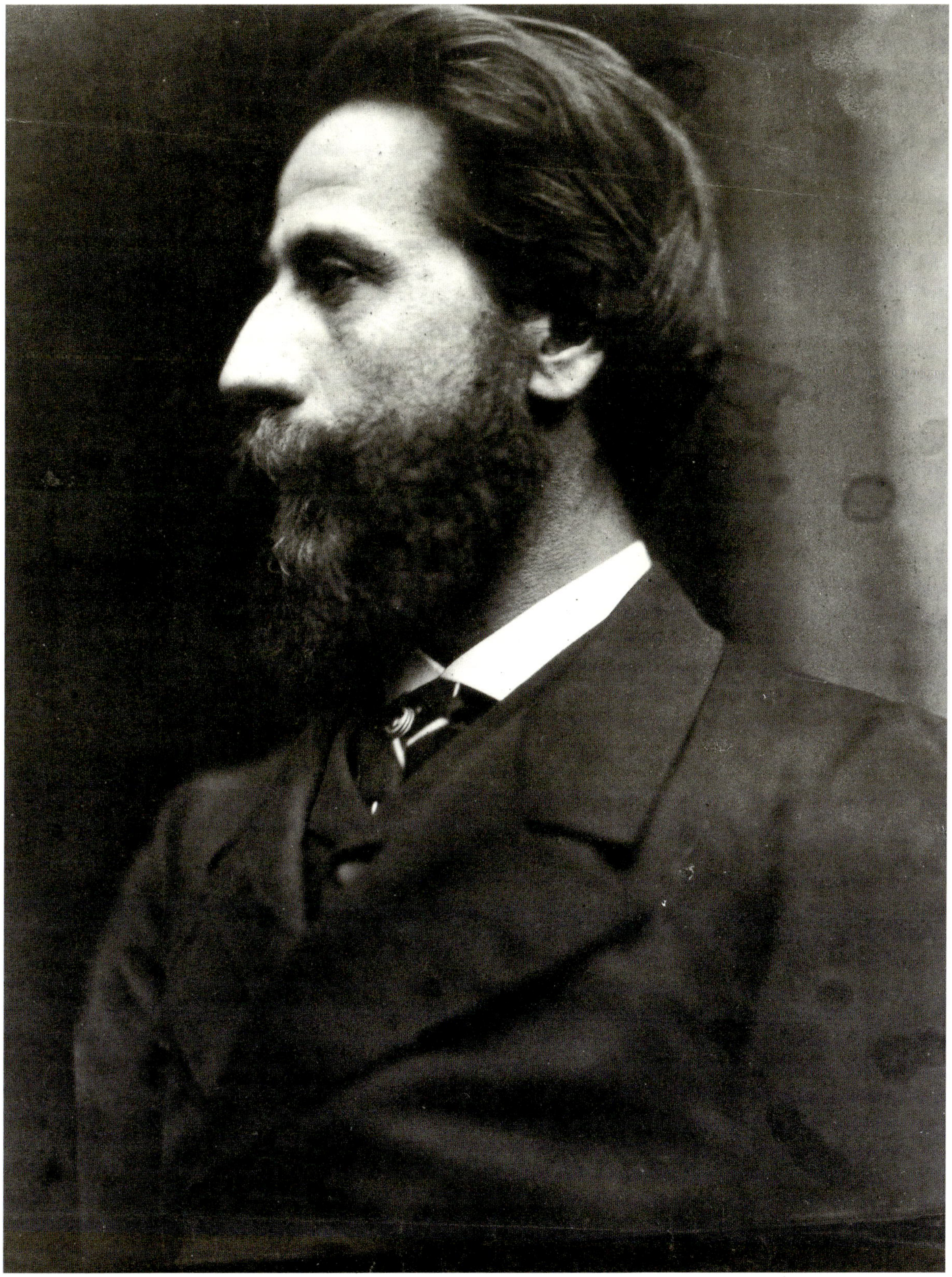

23 D.W. Wynfield, *Henry Tanworth Wells (1828–1903)*, undated (1860s), albumen print, 212 × 164mm, Royal Academy of Arts.

Patrons, Dilettantes and Inspirational Figures

Thomas Heatherley succeeded James Leigh at the art school in Newman Street in 1860. Wynfield photographed Heatherley, known for his solemn, monk-like appearance, in profile with his head bowed and his hands clasped together. The portrait is very different from Samuel Butler's irreverent painting *Mr Heatherley's Holiday* of 1873 (Tate Gallery, London) in which the director is shown mending the school skeleton after it had been damaged in a student prank. Under both Leigh and Heatherley amateur theatricals and fancy-dress balls were a feature of extra-curricular socialising.

Despite the tendency of Wynfield's contemporaries to pose as noblemen, those who were socially privileged found it difficult to be taken seriously as painters. Arthur Lewis was better known as a host than as an artist. His salons at Moray Lodge on Campden Hill became increasingly glittering and fashionable; in 1863 Du Maurier wrote to his mother that 'half the peerage will be there tonight and very likely the Prince of Wales' (*Letters*, p. 118). Du Maurier first met that other 'swell', the amateur artist Coutts Lindsay, in 1862 at Little Holland House, the atmosphere of which he found somewhat louche. Little is known about Edward King-Harman, a colonel who later became an Irish M.P.; a founder member of the Arts Club, he may have been a patron.

Wynfield's portrait of James Anthony Froude in a Puritan-style collar suggests that the artist and the historian saw their projects as sympathetic. Wynfield and the other historical genre painters of the rising school certainly perceived their use of historically accurate sources as a moral counterweight to the fanciful aspect of recreating 'the lost pages of history'. The scholarly approach of the younger generation was noted with approval by Francis Turner Palgrave who reserved his highest praise for those works which displayed 'a total absence of showiness and studio effect' (*Essays*, p.64).

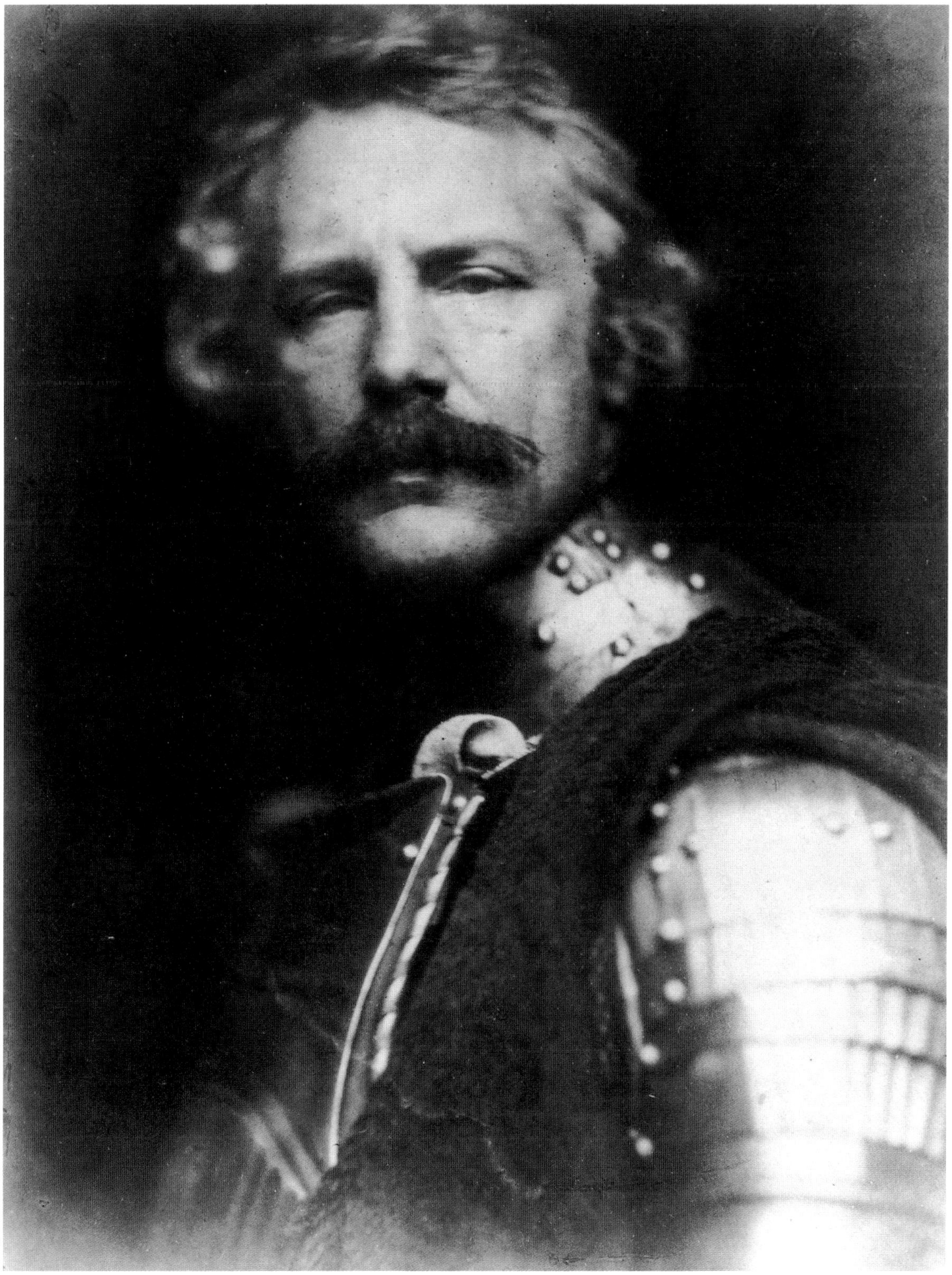

24 D.W. Wynfield, *Coutts Lindsay (1824–1913)*, undated (1860s), albumen print, 202 × 157mm, Royal Academy of Arts.

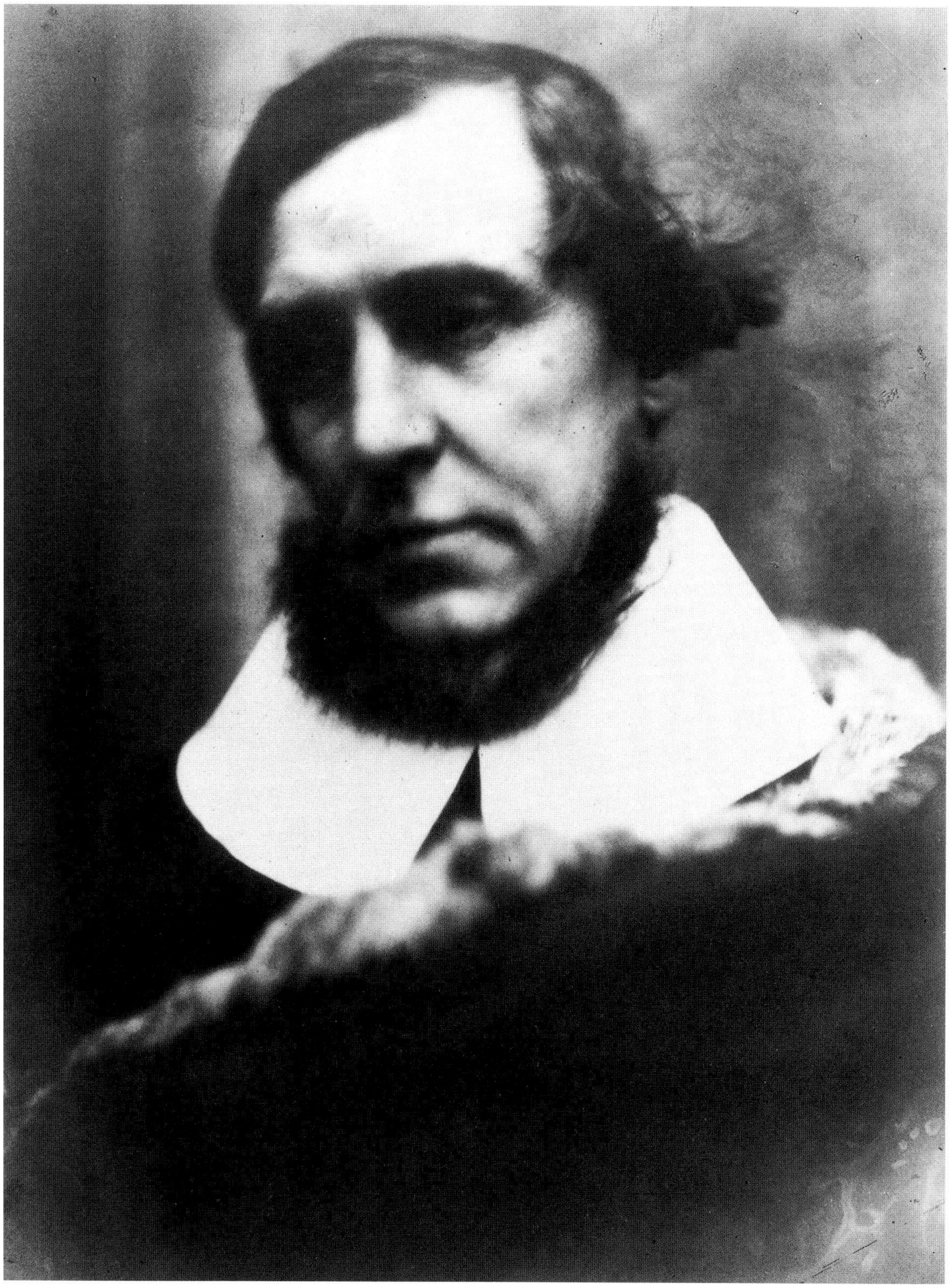

25 D.W. Wynfield, *James Anthony Froude (1818–1894)*, undated (1860s), albumen print, 200 × 153mm, Royal Academy of Arts.

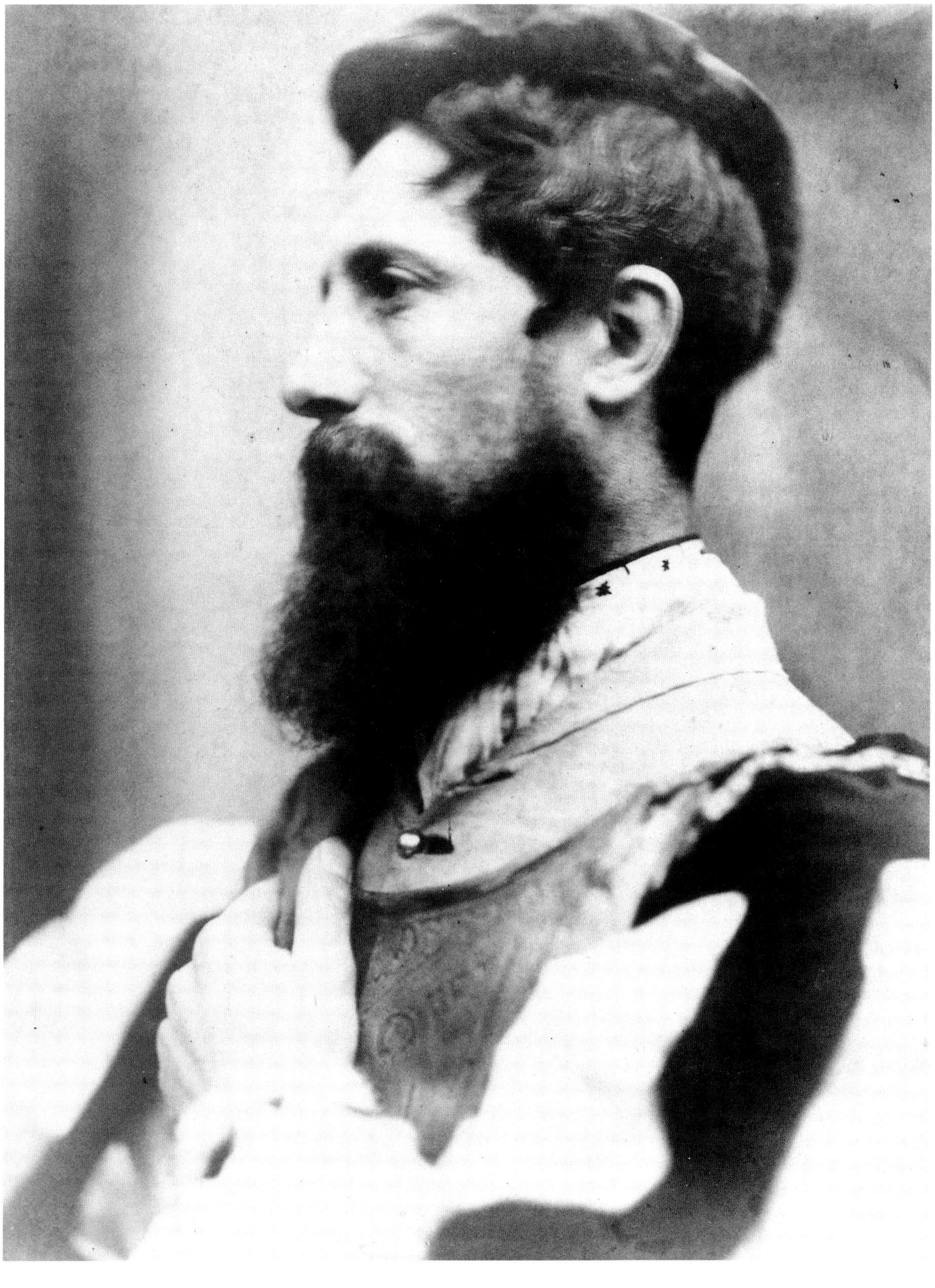

26 D.W. Wynfield, *Arthur Lewis (1824–1901)*, undated (1860s), albumen print, 219 × 160mm, Royal Academy of Arts.

The Pre-Raphaelites and After

In 1864, the year in which Wynfield published *The Studio*, Millais was the most famous contemporary artist of the day. He was also, according to George Du Maurier, as 'beautiful as a young god' (*Letters*, p.99). It was in the late 1850s that Millais first broke with the precepts of Pre-Raphaelitism by loosening his brushwork and changing his palette. William Holman Hunt, on the other hand, was determined to remain faithful to many precepts of the creed which they had formulated in 1848. Robert Braithwaite Martineau, the only known follower of Hunt's painstaking methods of composition and execution, also sat to Wynfield.

Burne-Jones was one of the many young men who became artists under the influence of Dante Gabriel Rossetti. He and Valentine Prinsep both contributed to the mural scheme for the Oxford Union executed under Rossetti's direction. This project is generally credited as being the first manifestation of the second phase of Pre-Raphaelitism upon which Rossetti was the dominant influence. Burne-Jones' unique admixture of medieval and early Renaissance forms seemingly produced without recourse to the study of nature were later vilified by the establishment as perverse and affected. The same terms were also used to denigrate the dream-like compositions of Simeon Solomon, the object of which appeared to be the celebration of artifice, decadence and sensuality.

Despite his admiration for Rossetti and the other Pre-Raphaelites, Valentine Prinsep's paintings were closest in spirit to those of Frederic Leighton. 'Val' or 'Buzz', as he was known, was the son of Thoby and Sara Prinsep, the nephew of Julia Margaret Cameron and an honorary member of the St John's Wood Clique. Described by George Leslie as 'an ever welcome guest both in the highest circles of society and at the Bohemian supper parties of the fraternity of artists in St John's Wood' (*Inner Life*, p. 186), Prinsep was a pivotal figure for bringing artists from different groupings into contact with one another. Renowned for his physical strength, he is thought to have been the model for Taffy in Du Maurier's *Trilby*.

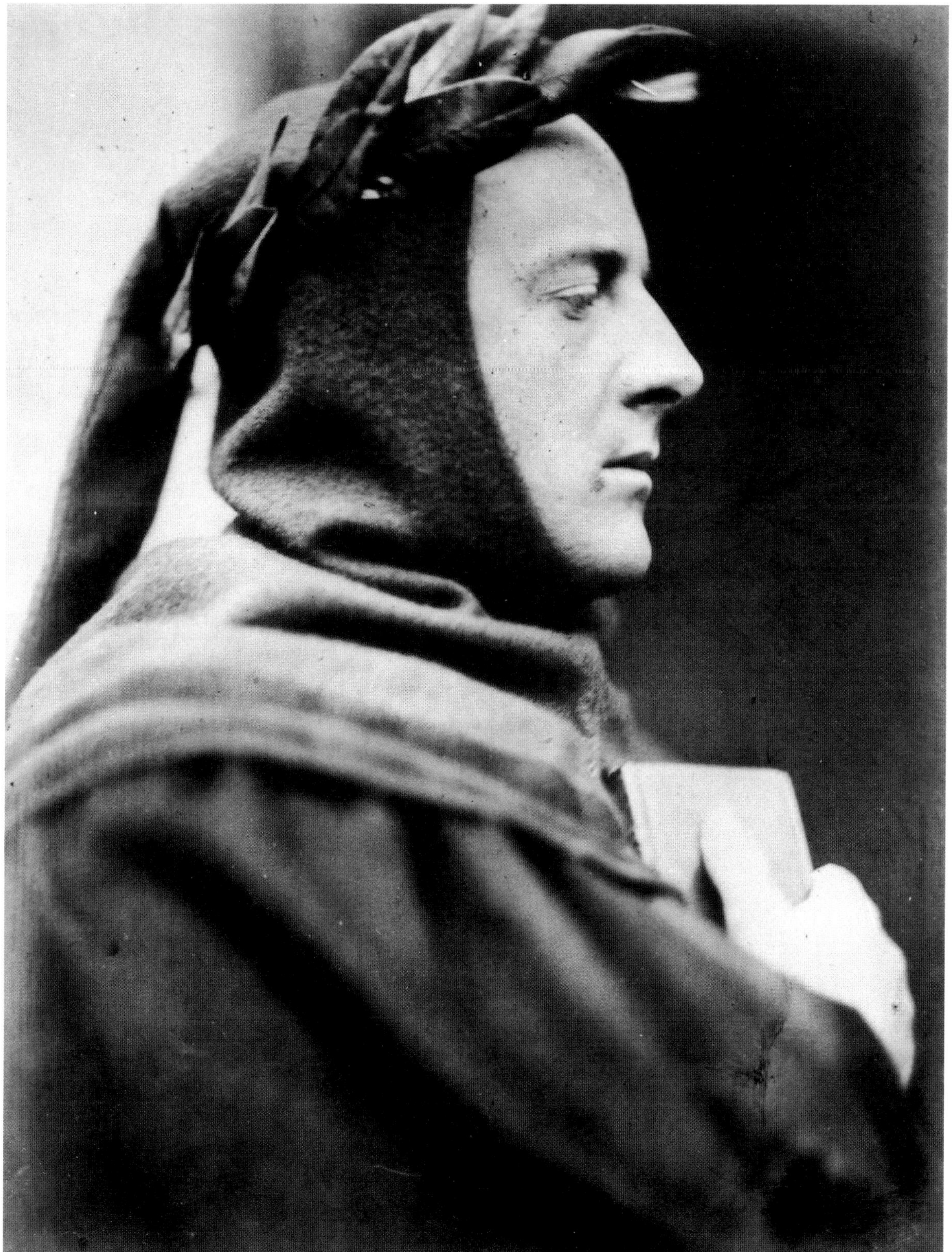

27 D.W. Wynfield, *John Everett Millais (1829–1896)*, undated (1860s), albumen print, 211 × 162mm, National Portrait Gallery.

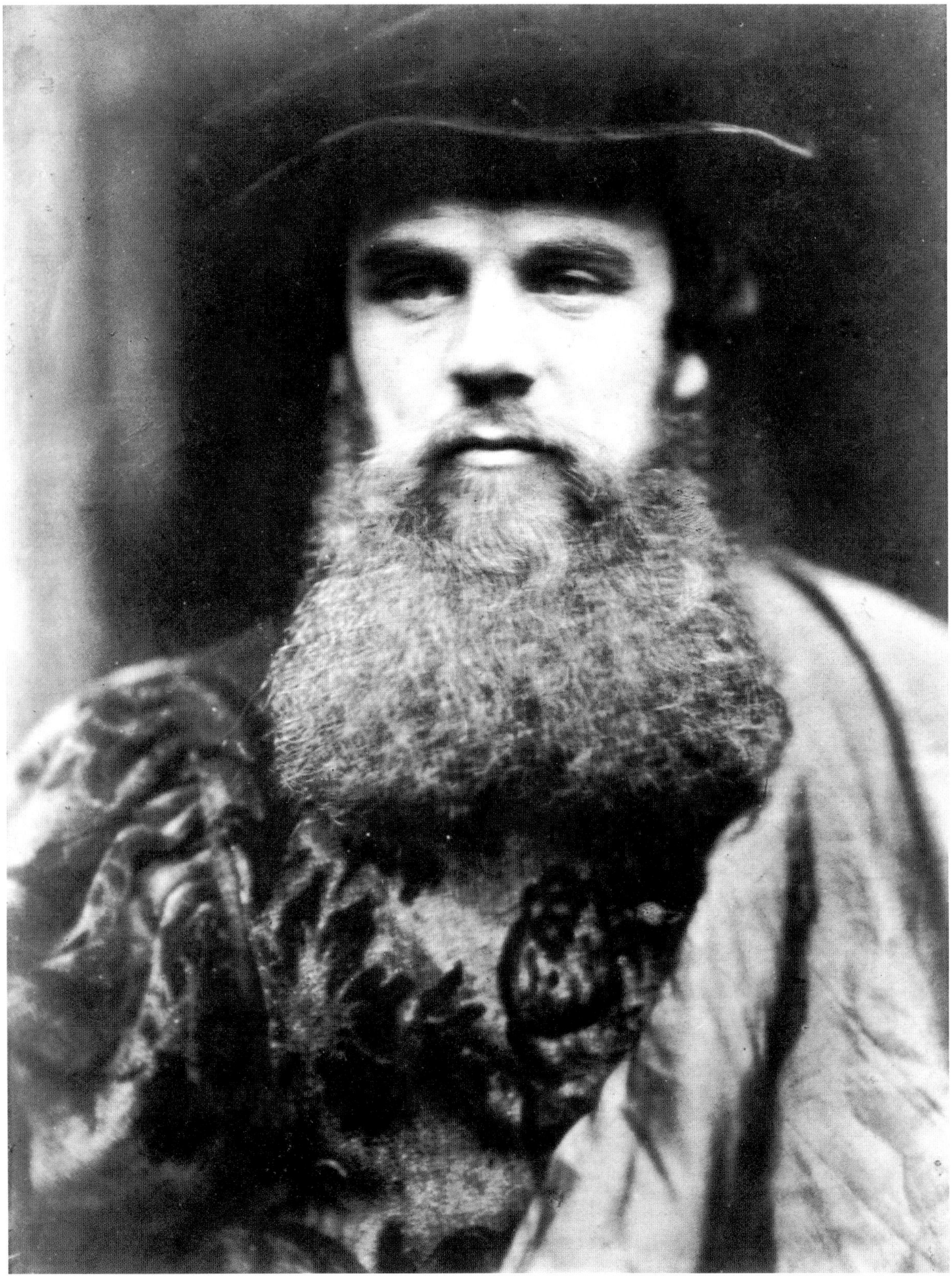

28 D.W. Wynfield, *William Holman Hunt (1827–1910), in Tudor costume*, undated (1860s), albumen print, 213 × 163mm, National Portrait Gallery.

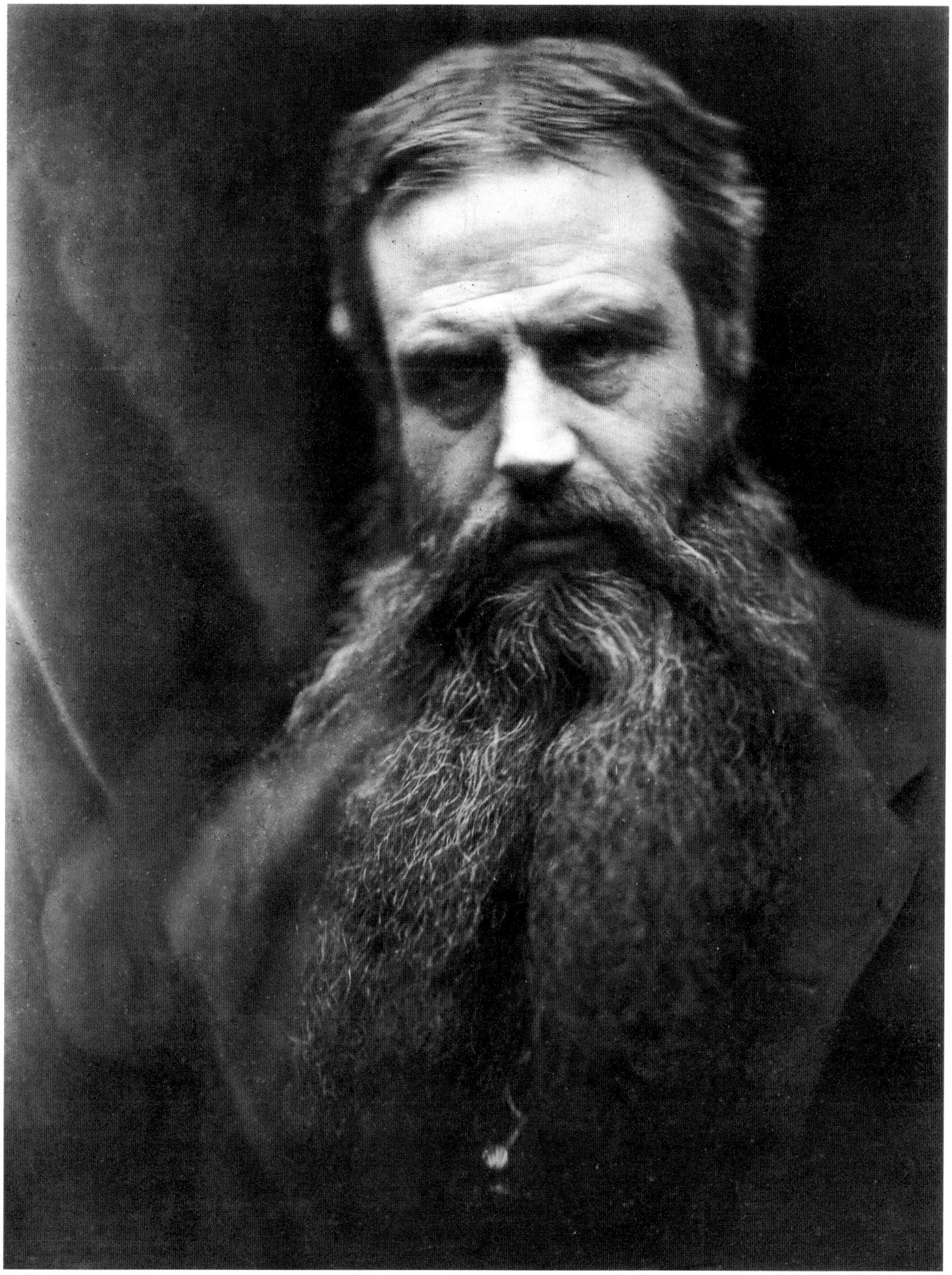

29 D.W. Wynfield, *William Holman Hunt (1827–1910), in contemporary dress*, undated (1870s?), albumen print, 212 × 165mm, Royal Academy of Arts.

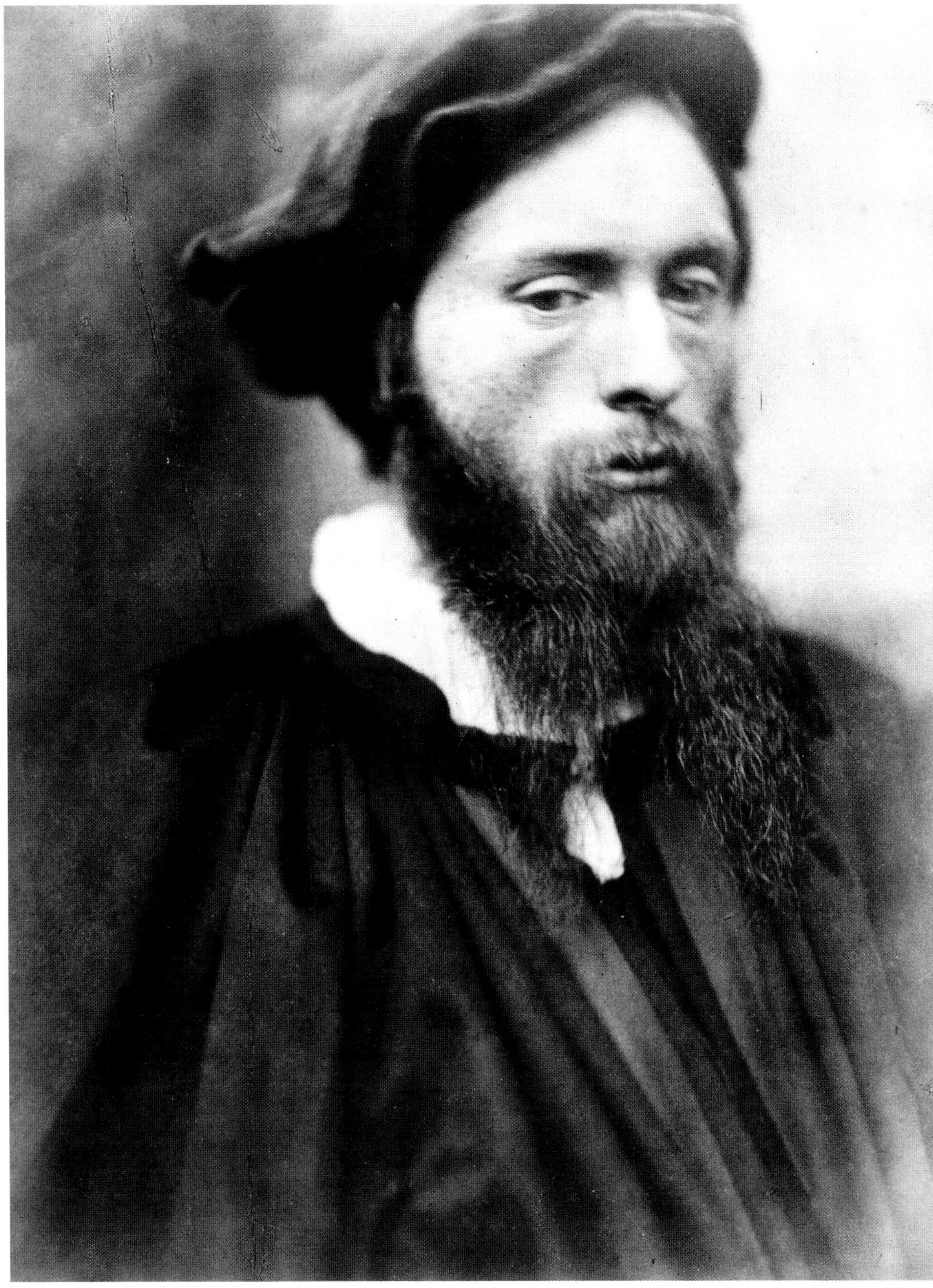

30 D.W. Wynfield, *Edward Burne-Jones (1833–1898), in three-quarters profile,* undated (1860s), albumen print, 211 × 161mm, Royal Academy of Arts.

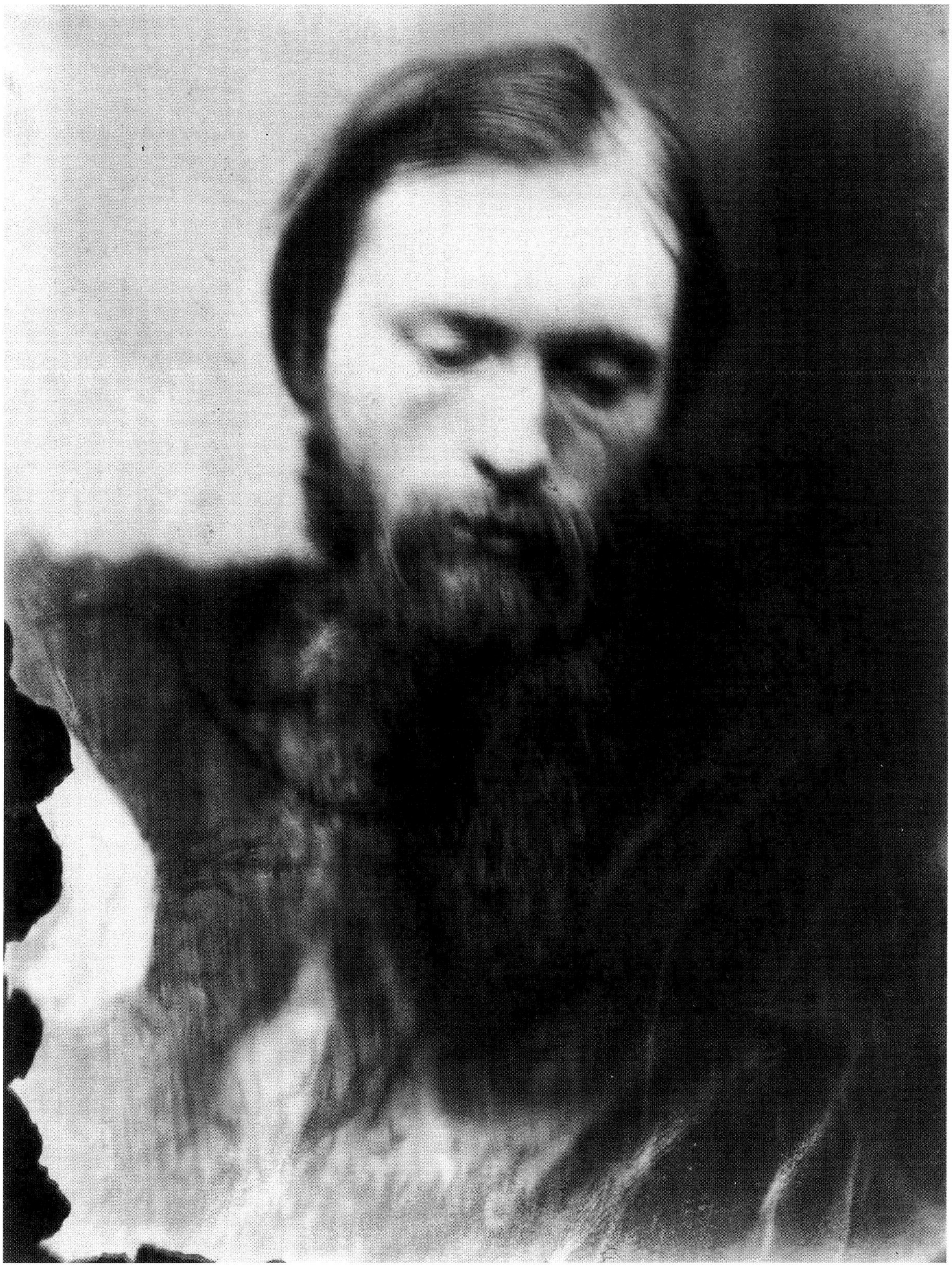

31 D.W. Wynfield, *Edward Burne-Jones (1883–1898), full face*, undated (1860s), albumen print, 209 × 163mm, Royal Academy of Arts.

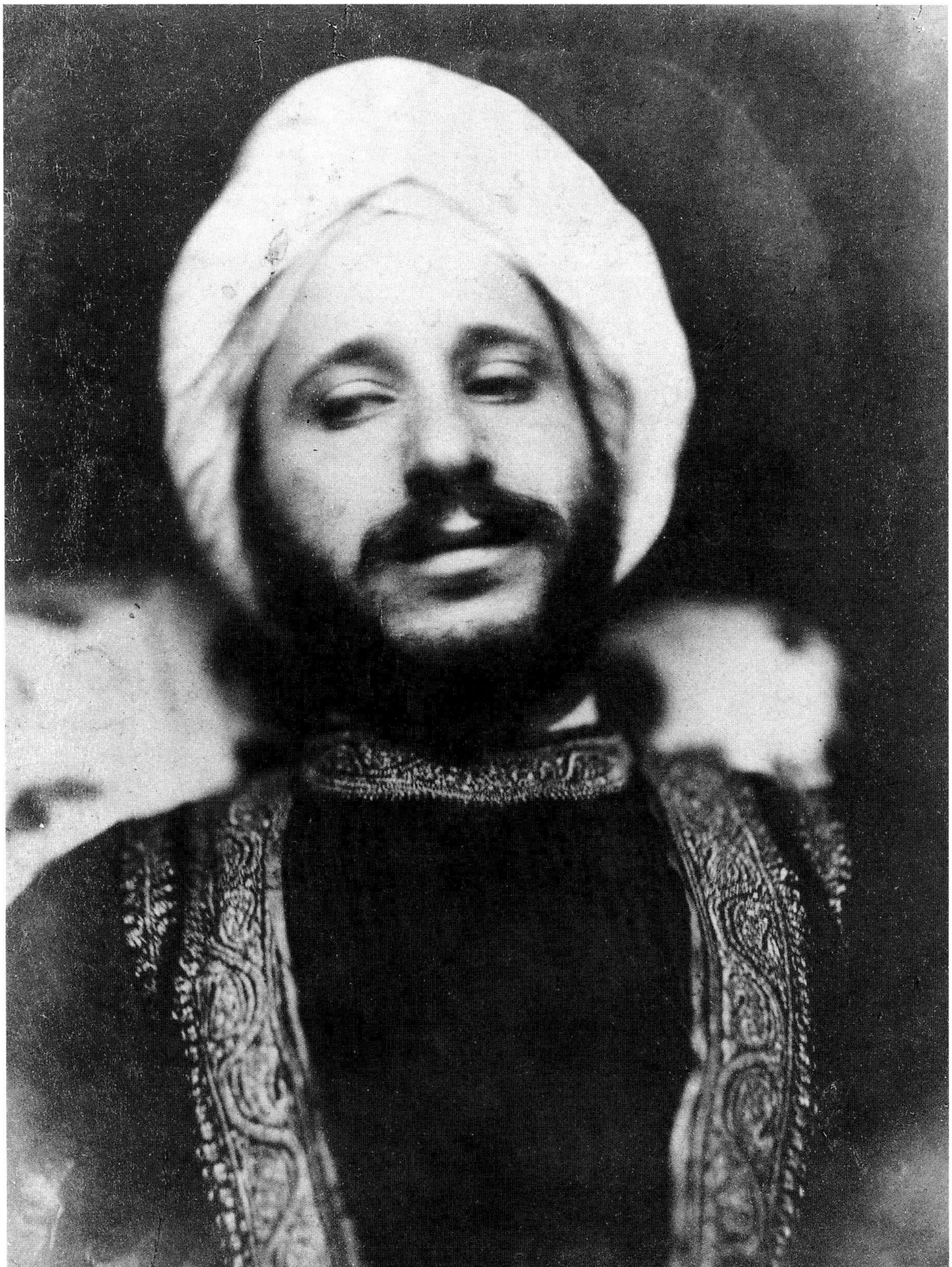

32 D.W. Wynfield, *Simeon Solomon (1840–1905)*, undated (1860s), albumen print, 202 × 151mm, Royal Academy of Arts.

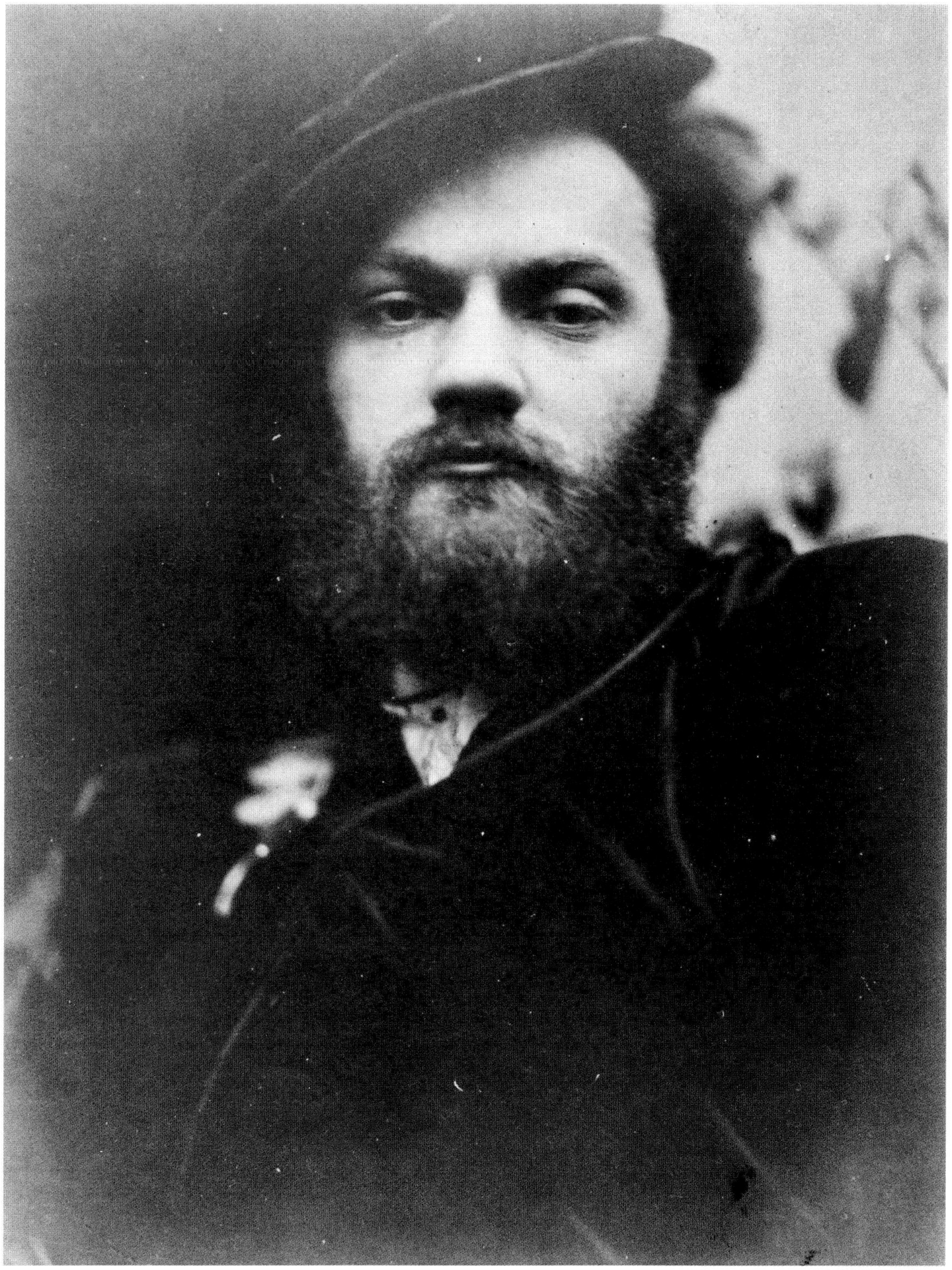

33 D.W. Wynfield, *Valentine Cameron Prinsep (1838–1904)*, undated (1860s), albumen print, 206 × 160mm, Royal Photographic Society.

The New Masters

In 1855 a whole wall in the West Room of the Royal Academy was occupied by one painting, *Cimabue's Madonna is Carried in Procession through the Streets of Florence*. This was the work of Frederic Leighton, an artist then hardly known in Britain, and had been painted in Rome. Although the critics were divided as to its merits it was bought by the Queen for the Royal Collection and the twenty-five-year-old Leighton, who had studied art in Frankfurt and Florence, became the object of intense interest.

Leighton could have painted in imitation of any school of art that he chose but he instead developed an eclectic style which drew upon the dominant traditions of western art: medieval and classical, romantic and naturalistic, northern and southern European. His *Dante in Exile* of 1864 (private collection) was an exercise in the play of opposites: the Florentine Dante's encounter with the colour and pageantry of Verona symbolises an exchange between Florentine design and Northern Italian colouring and brushwork. This painting, exhibited together with *Golden Hours* at the Royal Academy in 1864, overcame the opposition to Leighton's work within the Academy and secured his election as an associate.

Despite Leighton's aspirations to master both line and colour he was widely acknowledged as a finer draughtsman than colourist. It was left to George Frederic Watts to play Titian to his Cimabue. Watts first came to the attention of the British public in 1843 when he won a prize for his design for the decorative scheme of the new Houses of Parliament entitled *Caractacus Led in Triumph through the Streets of Rome*. Despite the failure of the Houses of Parliament scheme to revive painting in the grand manner, Watts dedicated his life to the ideals, and occasionally the production, of High Art. The portraits which he produced for his 'Hall of Fame' scheme, the majority of which are now in the National Portrait Gallery, are both a testament to the Victorian belief that great men embodied the spirit of the age and formal exercises in Venetian colouring.

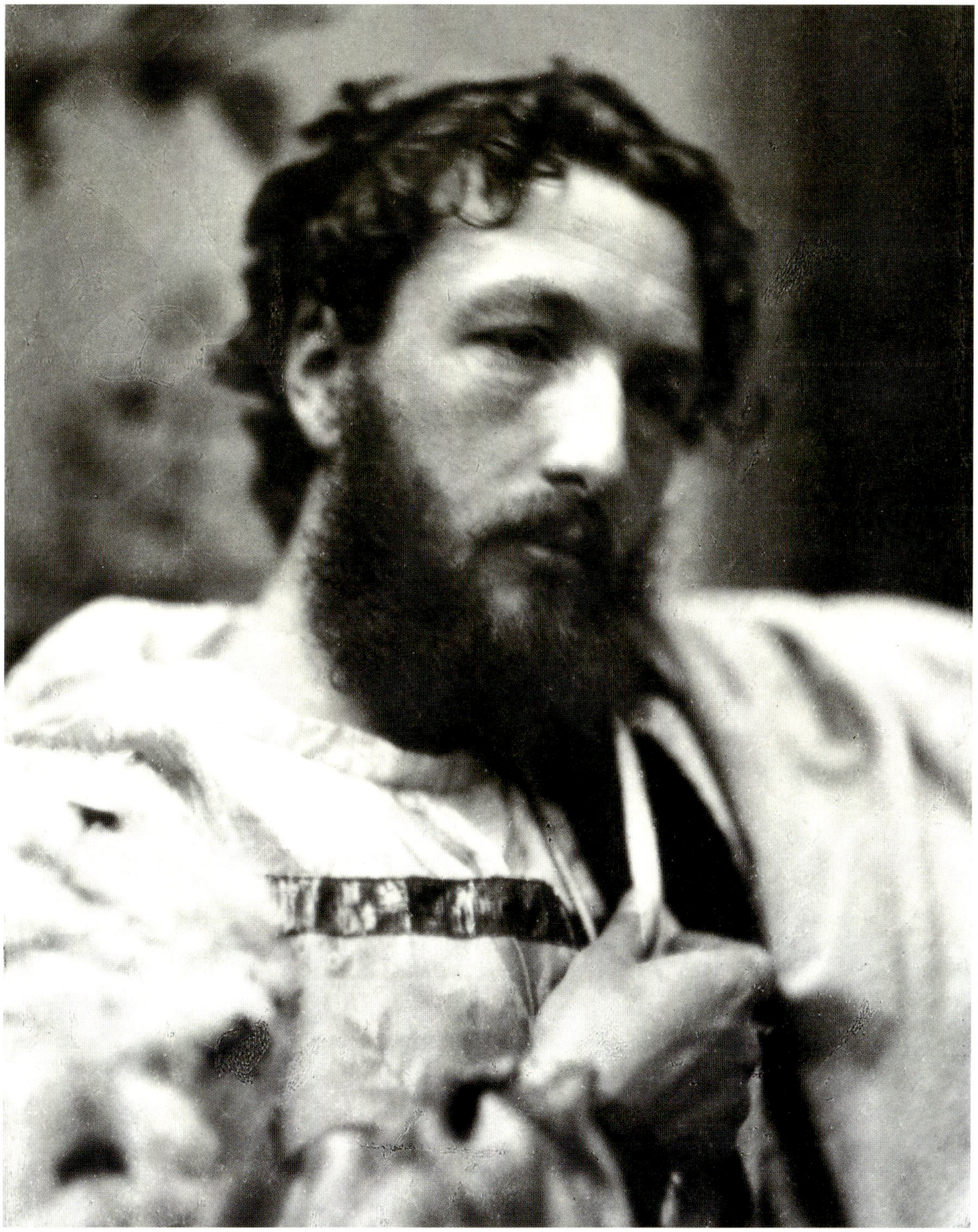

34 D.W. Wynfield, *Frederic Leighton (1830–1896), in three-quarters profile*, undated (1860s), carbon print, 192 × 158mm, Royal Academy of Arts.

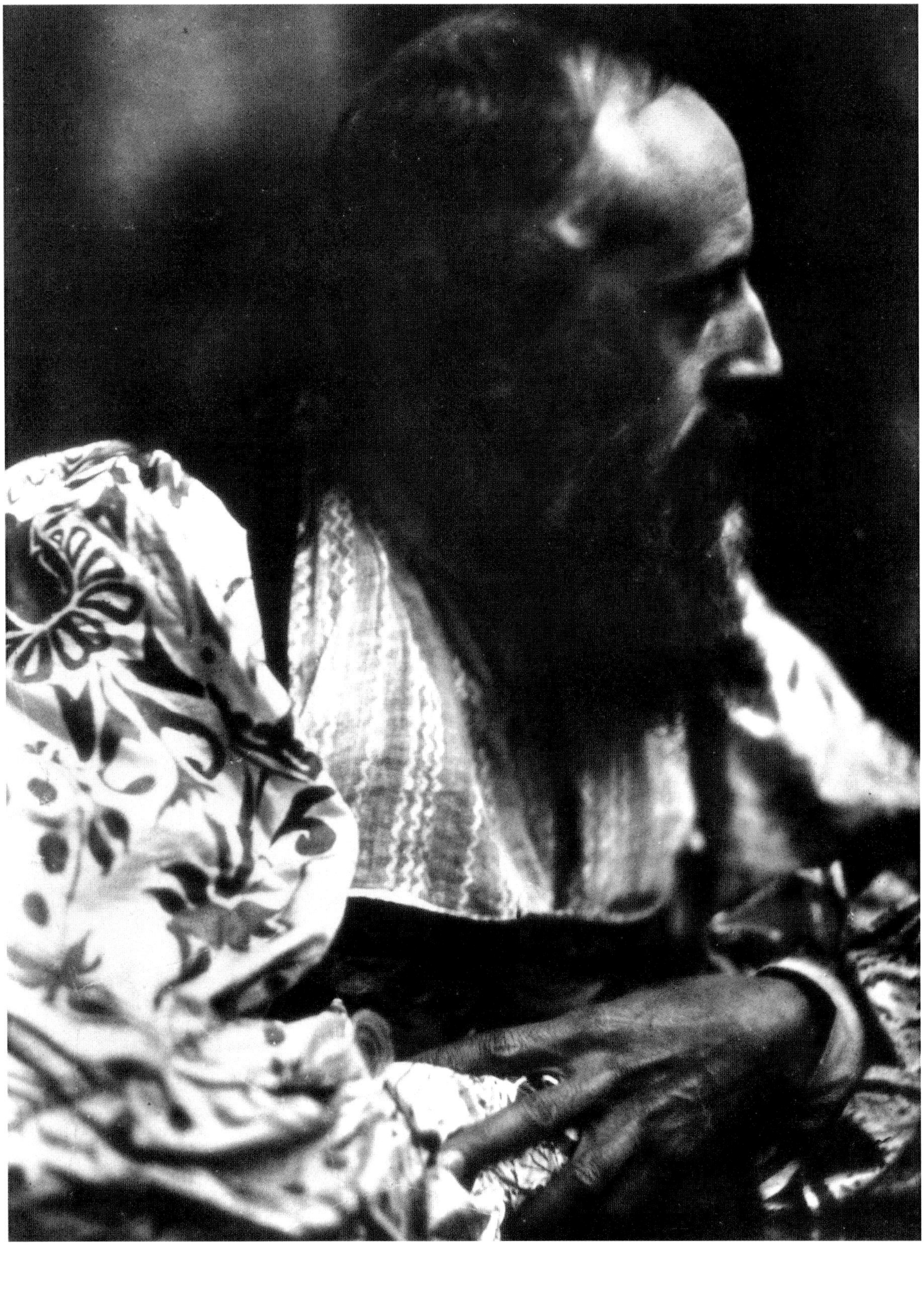

35 D.W. Wynfield, *George Frederic Watts (1817–1904)*, undated (1860s), carbon print, 211 × 162mm, Royal Academy of Arts.

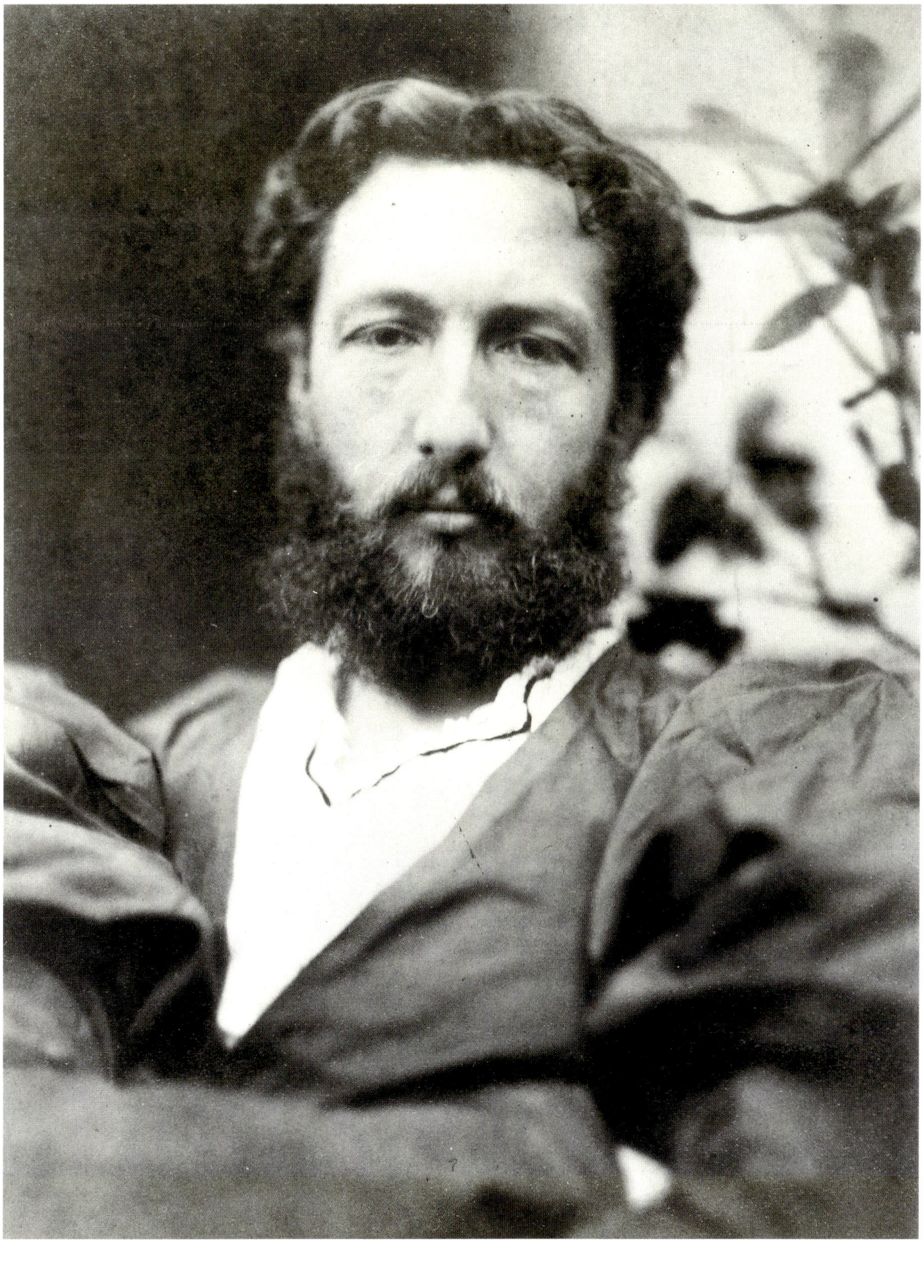

36 D.W. Wynfield, *Frederic Leighton (1830–1896), full-face portrait*, undated (1860s), albumen print, 213 × 162mm, National Portrait Gallery.

Foreign Exchanges

Although we cannot be certain that Wynfield's portrait of Manet was taken in London and not Paris, there is no evidence to suggest that Wynfield ever visited the French capital. The meeting of these two men apparently polarised by their aesthetic creeds signifies the success of Wynfield's rising generation in establishing their influence over alternative venues of exhibition to the Royal Academy in the second half of the 1860s.

Manet had submitted two paintings to the Royal Academy in 1865 but neither of them were exhibited. Undeterred by this experience he visited London in 1868 and wrote to Henri Fantin-Latour on his return:

> I believe there is something to be done over there — the feel of the place, the atmosphere, everything pleased me, and I'm going to try and show my work there next year — among other things you should exhibit my portrait — it would be good for both of us.

The portrait to which Manet refers is Fantin-Latour's 1867 depiction of him as the top-hatted *flâneur* (Art Institute, Chicago). In Wynfield's portrait of Manet the sitter's face does not compete for attention with his clothes and the viewer is transfixed by the intensity of Manet's gaze.

Manet's guide in London was Alphonse Legros who had followed Whistler in his move from Paris to London. Having fallen out with Whistler in 1867 Legros moved closer to his English contemporaries; in 1868, the year of Manet's visit, the work which he exhibited at the Royal Academy was entitled *Sir Thomas More showing Paintings by Holbein to Henry VIII*. Legros taught etching at the South Kensington School of Art and was an immensely significant figure in the graphic revival of the 1860s and 1870s.

William Wetmore Story is the only (identified) sculptor to sit to Wynfield. Born in Massachussetts and trained as a lawyer, Story left for Europe in 1856 where he practiced as a sculptor in the neo-classical tradition.

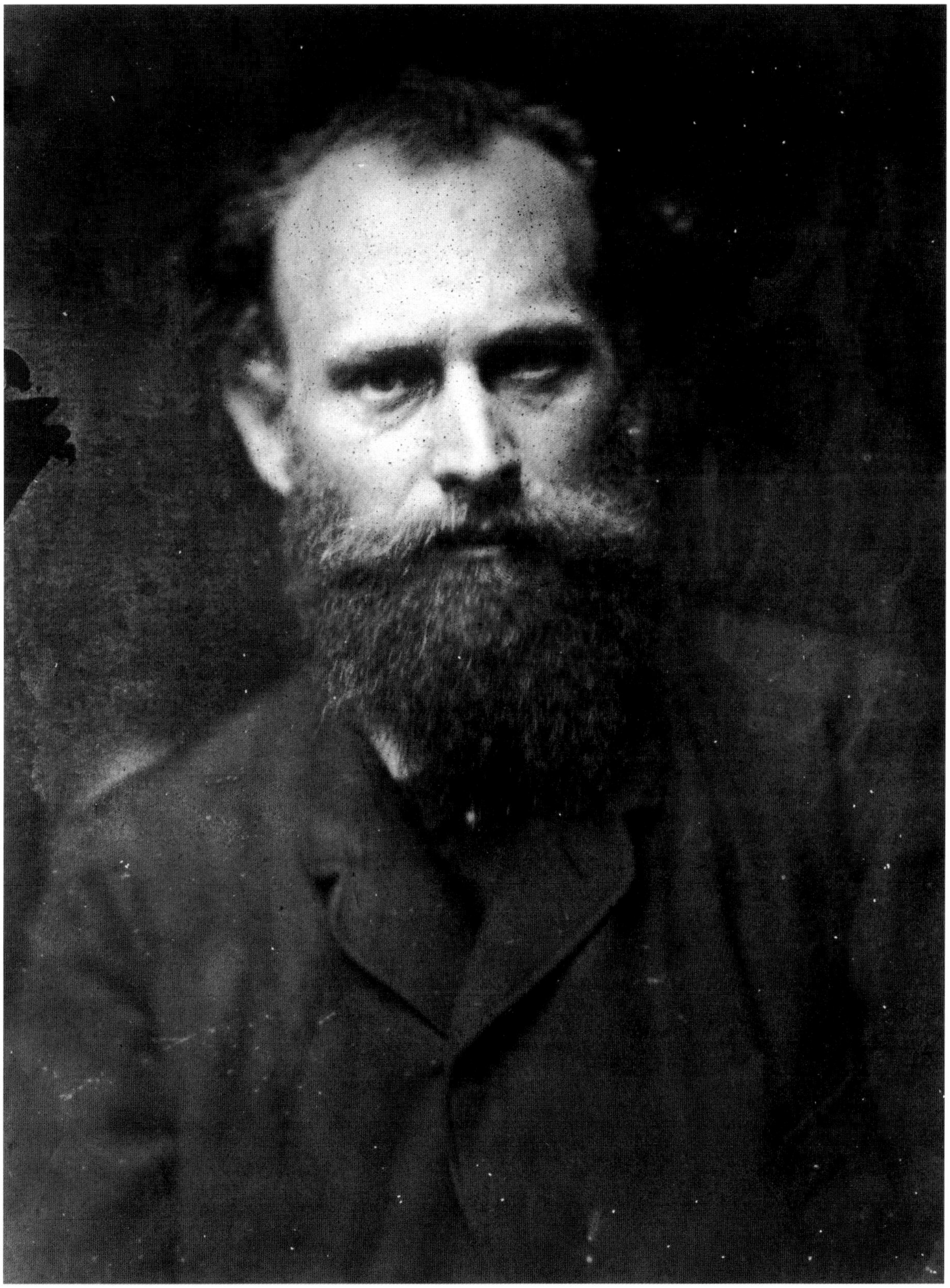

37 D.W. Wynfield, *Edouard Manet (1832–1883)*, undated (1868), albumen print, 216 × 166mm, Royal Academy of Arts.

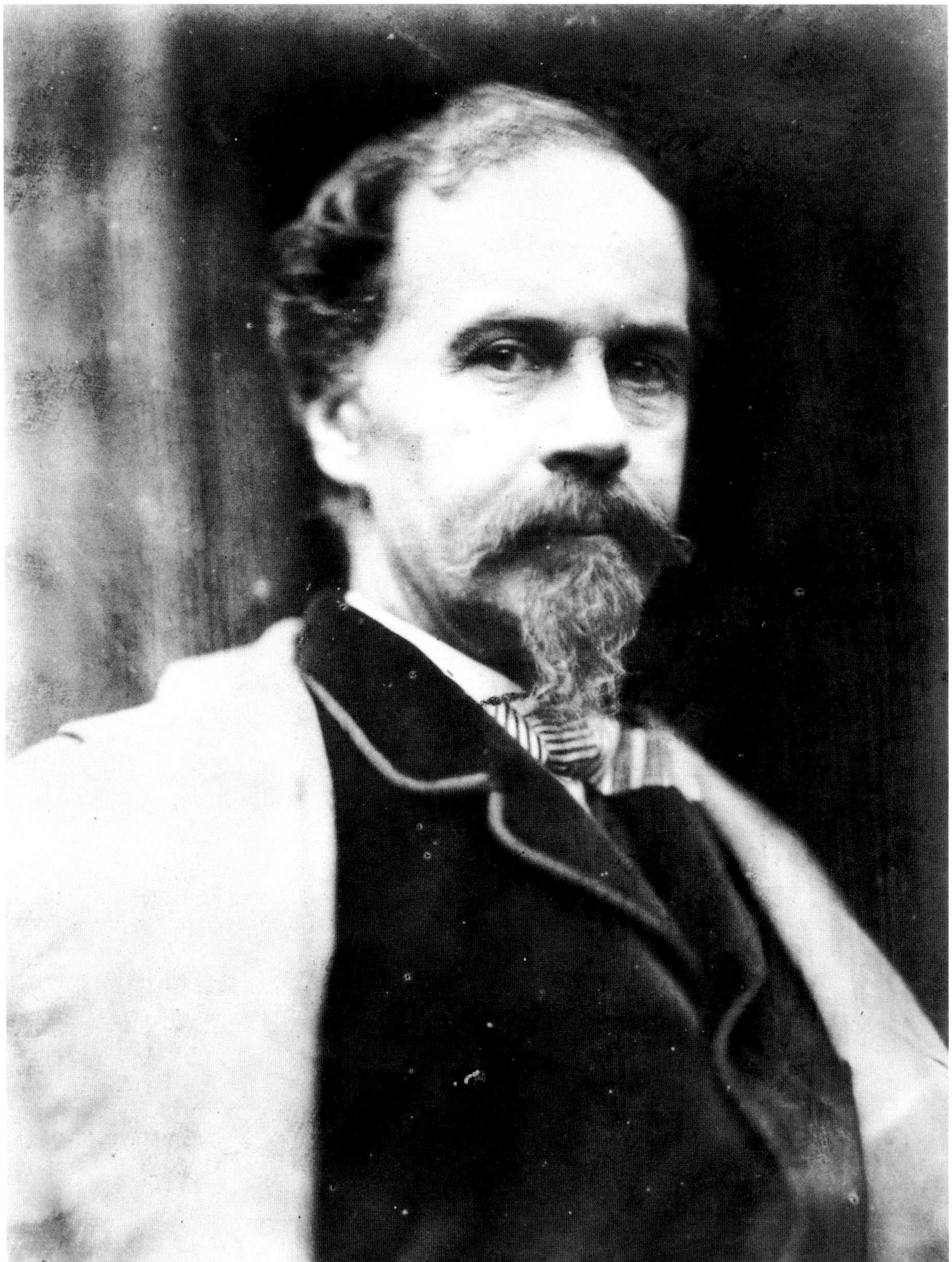

38 D.W. Wynfield, *William Wetmore Story (1819–1895)*, undated (1860s), albumen print, 213 × 162mm, Royal Photographic Society.

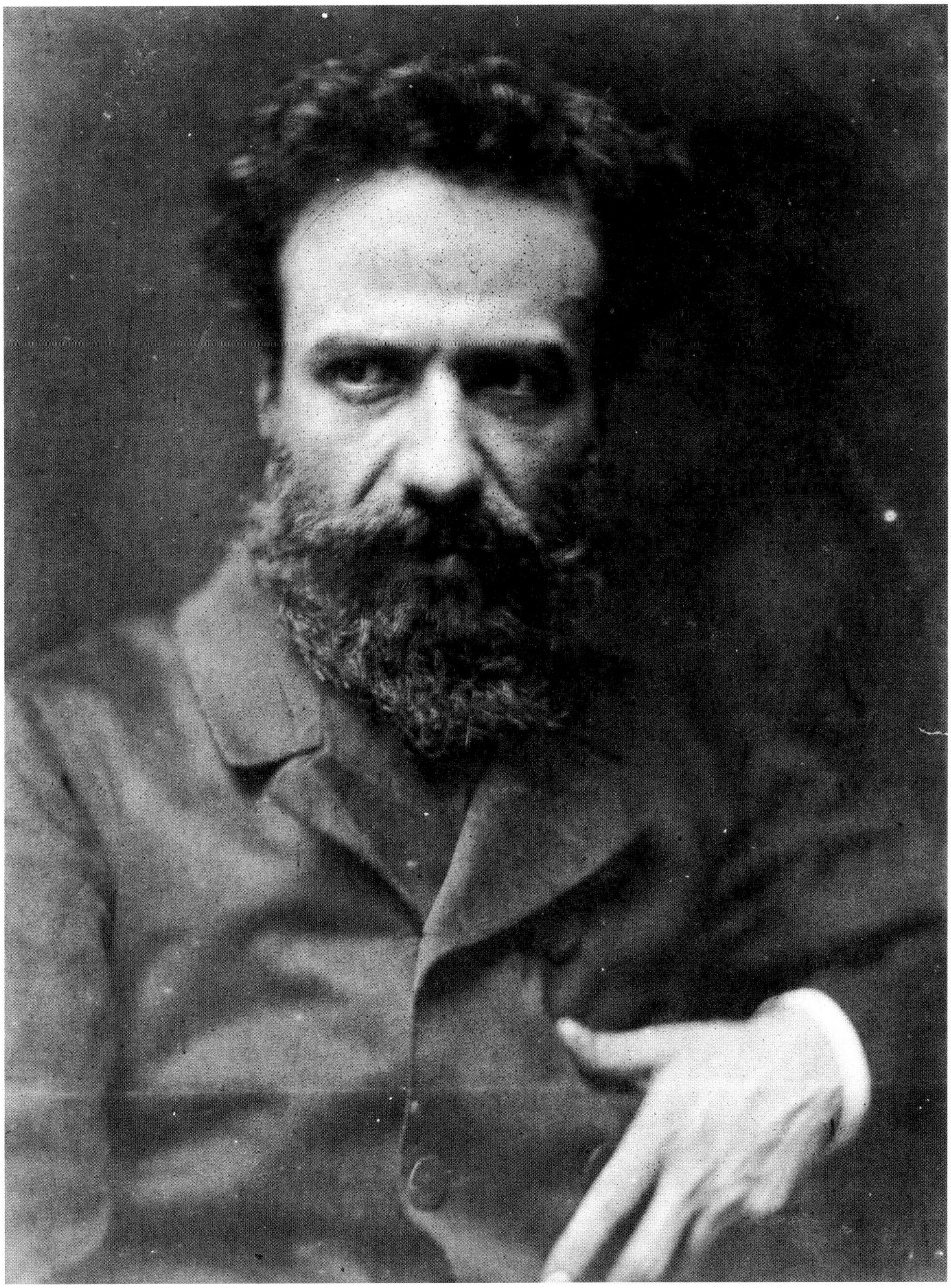

39 D.W. Wynfield, *Alphonse Legros (1837–1911)*, undated (1860s), albumen print, 213 × 163mm, Royal Academy of Arts.

Graphic Artists

The 1860s and 1870s was the golden age of graphic illustration in Britain. The massive expansion in the periodical press which followed the repeal of the stationery duty in the late 1850s provided many artists with a new source of income. The status of graphic art and of the graphic artist was elevated by the publication of the Moxon Tennyson in 1857 for which leading contemporary artists, including Millais, Holman Hunt and Rossetti, had supplied the illustrations. According to Du Maurier, by 1862 Millais was making £3,000 a year, £800 of which was from supplying designs to be wood-engraved (*Letters*, p.150).

The various sketching societies proved popular with the new generation of graphic artists who were required to improvise at short notice on a given humourous or literary subject. In 1860 Du Maurier's first cartoon for *Punch* was published and four years later he was taken on as a staff artist. Frederick Walker made his name with his illustrations to Thackeray's *The Adventures of Philip* which were published in the *Cornhill Magazine* in 1861–2. In the mid-1860s Walker distinguished himself as a watercolourist and then, at the end of the decade, as a social realist painter in oils. This 'genius', as he was often called by his contemporaries, died of tuberculosis at the age of thirty-four.

Despite the fact that they are known today for their illustrations, Frederic Shields, John Dawson Watson and Charles Keene were all painters as well as graphic artists. Keene was acclaimed by his artist contemporaries as one of the most talented, and underrated, artists of their generation. He also epitomised the idea of the English bohemian. Du Maurier said of him:

> His bohemian world was mine — and I found it a very good world and very much to my taste — a clean, honest, wholesome, innocent, intellectual and most industrious British bohemia, with lots of tobacco, lots of good music, plenty of talk about literature and art, and no too much victuals and drink.
> *Letters*, p. 278

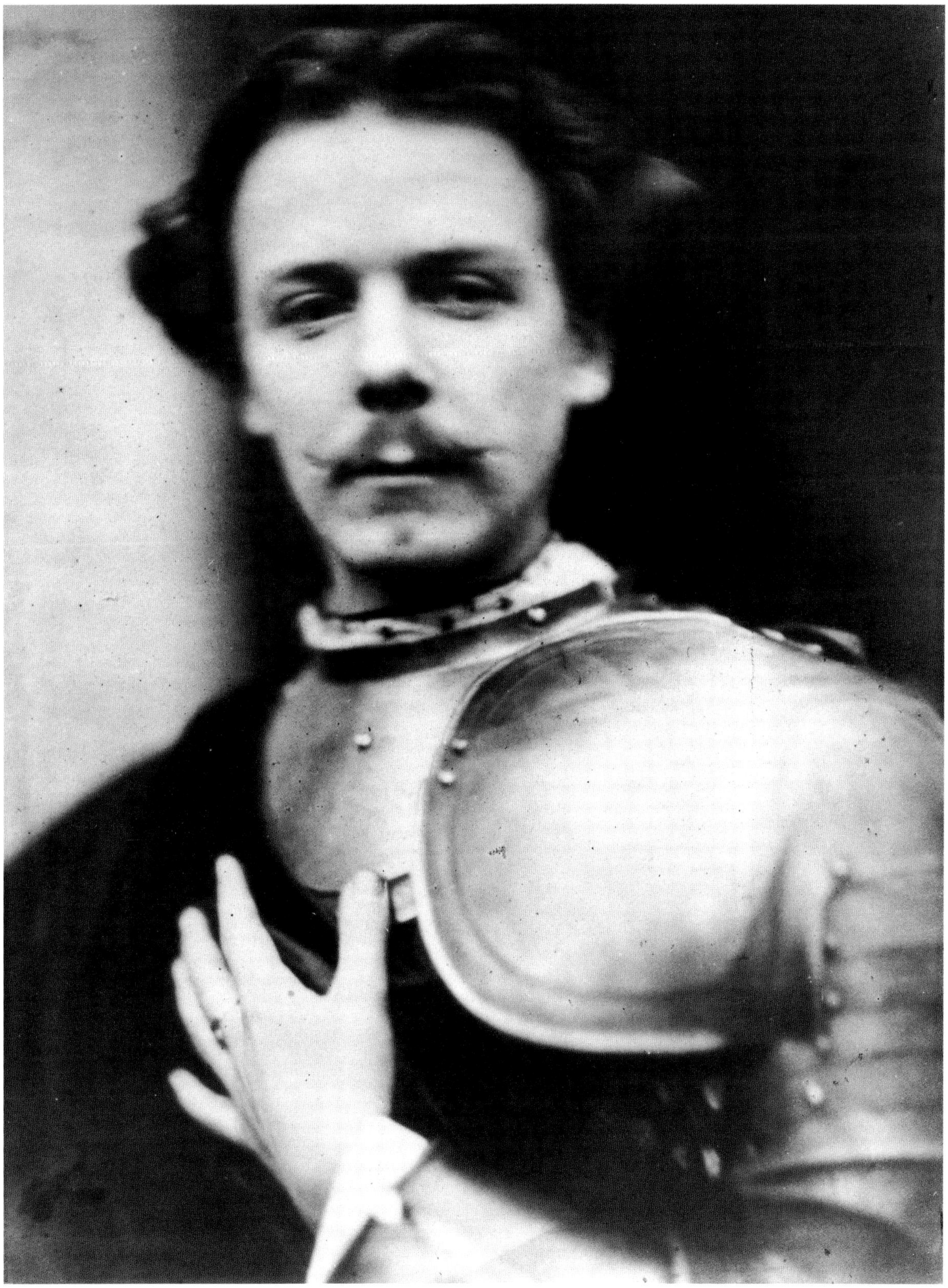

40 D.W. Wynfield, *George Du Maurier (1834–1896)*, undated (1860s), albumen print, 219 × 169mm, Royal Academy of Arts.

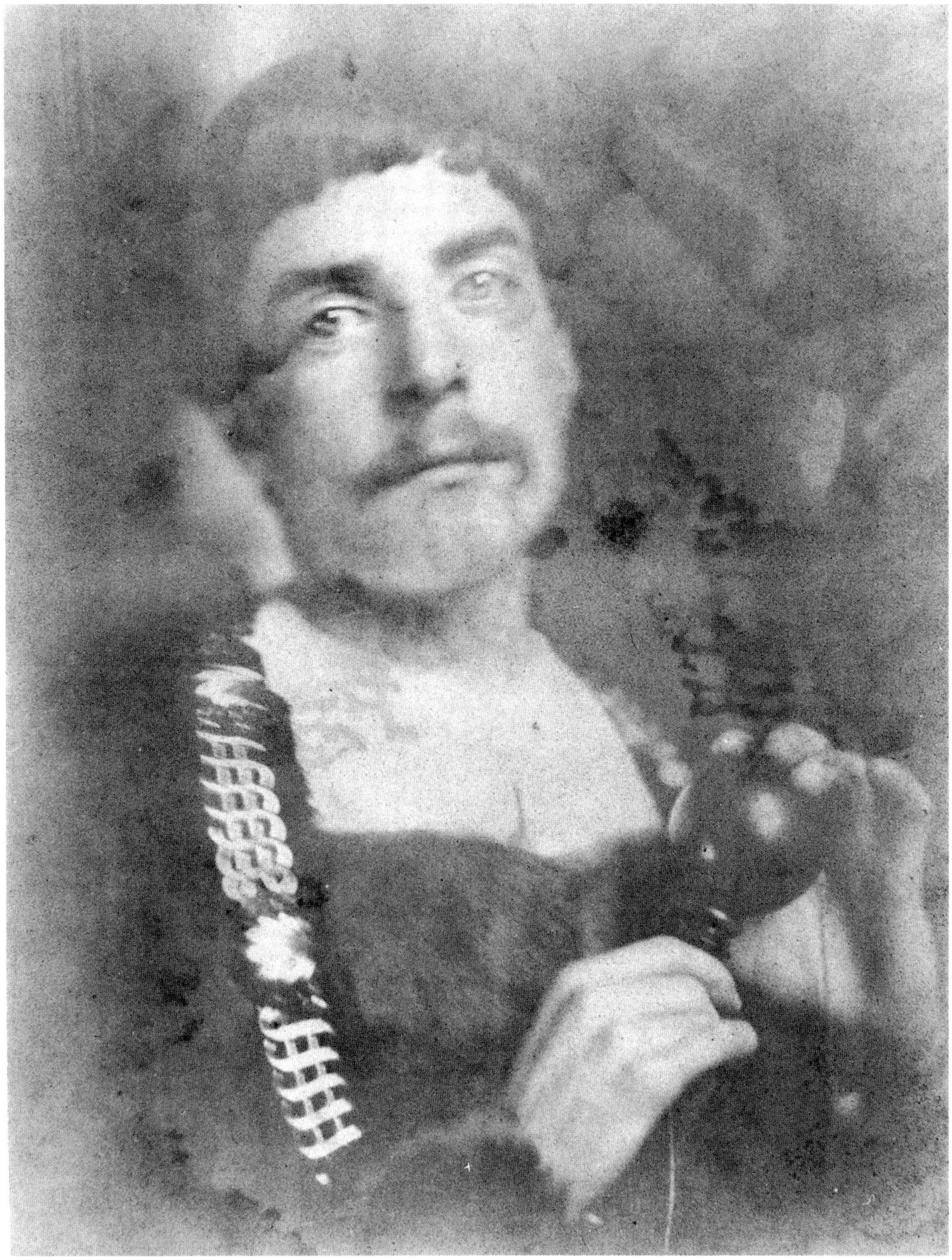

41 D.W. Wynfield, *Frederick Walker (1840–1875), full-face portrait*, undated (1860s), albumen print, 195 × 151mm, Royal Photographic Society.

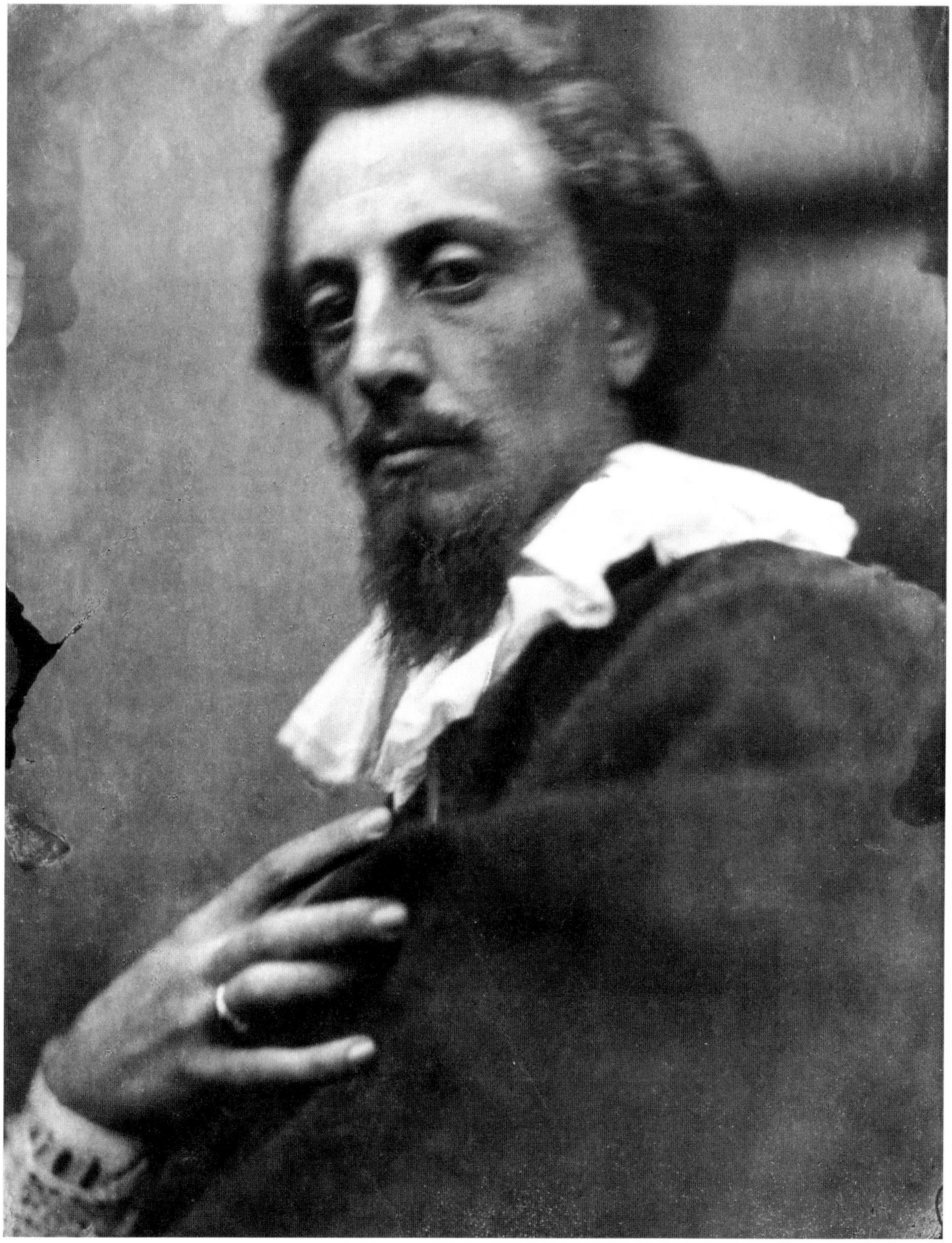

42 D.W. Wynfield, *John Dawson Watson (1832–1892), in falling collar*, undated (1860s), carbon print, 215 × 168mm, Royal Academy of Arts.

The Artist's Models

There is, so far, only one known photograph by Wynfield taken of a woman in his distinctive out-of-focus style. It is of Annie Yeames, Wynfield's sister and William Frederick Yeames' wife. There is another element to this photograph which makes it stand out from the others: the pose. The turn of Yeames' head away from the camera and the way in which she holds up a tray of apples suggests that this is less a portrait than a study in the manner of Titian.

This is not the only photograph which suggests that Wynfield may have used his camera to produce studies for his paintings. It is possible that the two unidentified young men photographed by Wynfield were either professional or casual models. The fair-haired sitter was at one time identified as a lifeguardsman, and it is known that some members of London's military barracks did pose for artists. The fact that this sitter does not sport a bushy beard further suggests that he was not an artist. According to Philip Gilbert Hamerton:

> It was not by any means accidental that the beard movement should have originated with artists, who, however artificial their pursuit may be in itself, are brought more into contact with real nature, and are more observant of its beauties, than any other class of persons. On the other hand, shaving had generally formed part of the idea aimed at by disciplined professions, such as those of the soldier, the lawyer and the priest.
> *Portfolio Papers*, 1889, pp. 189–90

Despite the fact that these two sitters do not wear the 'toga virilis', as the beard was jokingly referred to, they do not look out of place in Wynfield's series. Wynfield's appreciation of different types of masculine beauty is evident; whether that appreciation was sexual as well as aesthetic is not. A fragment of a letter which has been preserved among the papers belonging to W.F. Yeames may or may not refer to Wynfield:

> The thing amused me much in David's epistle he winds up by stating that *women know nothing*[.] I [illegible]of it Master David and if you only live long enough my dear boy you will acknowledge that they do know something aye and will teach it to you perhaps if you are so disposed.

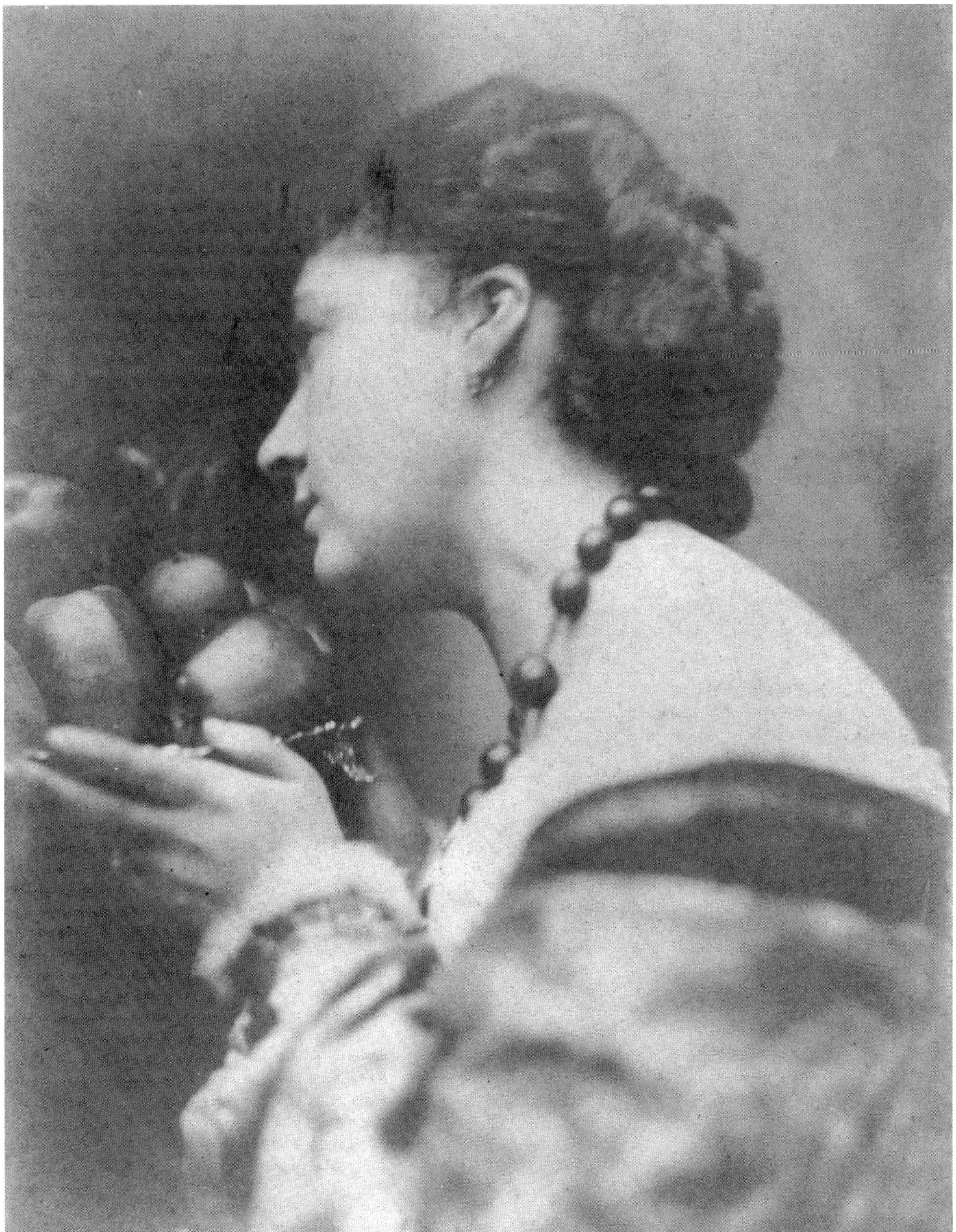

43 D.W. Wynfield, *Annie Yeames*, née *Winfield*, undated (1860s), albumen print, 215 × 169mm, Royal Photographic Society.

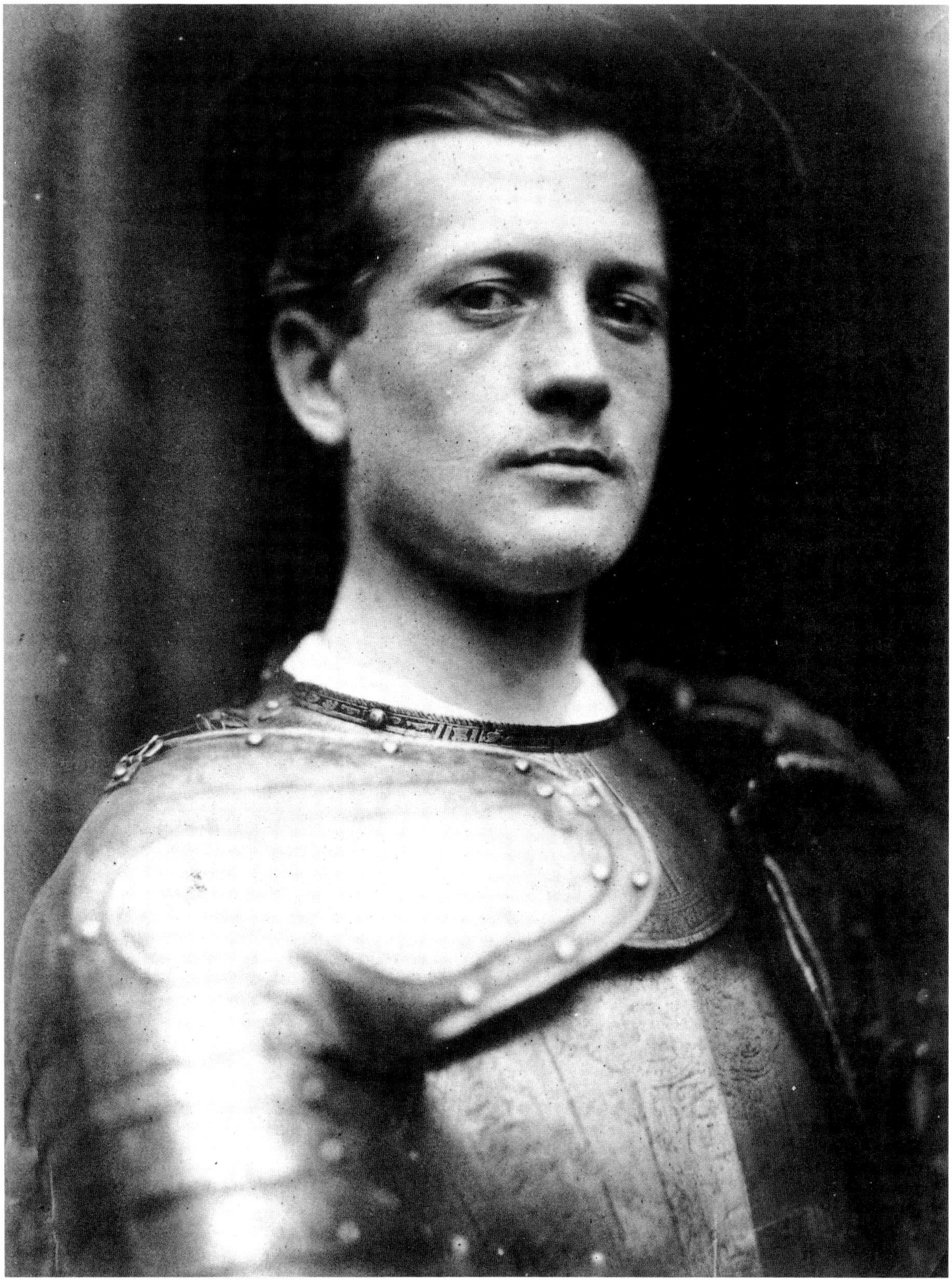

44 D.W. Wynfield, *Unidentified man*, undated (1860s), albumen print, 212 × 163mm, Royal Academy of Arts.

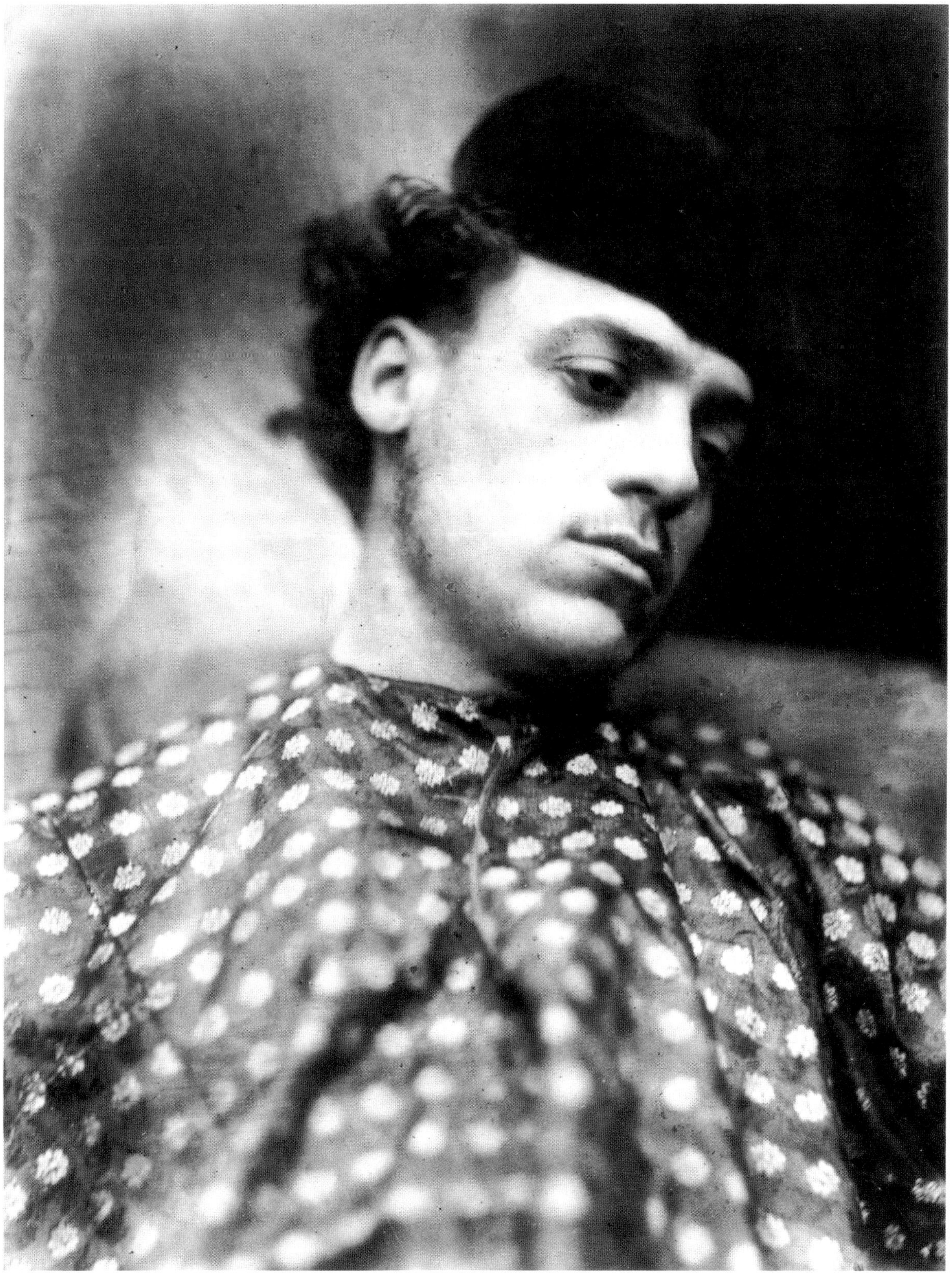

45 D.W. Wynfield, *Unidentified man*, undated (1860s), albumen print, 213 × 163mm, Royal Academy of Arts.

List of Plates

22 D.W. Wynfield, *Field Talfourd (1814–1874)*, undated (1860s), albumen print, 215 × 163mm, Royal Academy of Arts.

23 D.W. Wynfield, *Henry Tanworth Wells (1828–1903)*, undated (1860s), albumen print, 212 × 164mm, Royal Academy of Arts.

24 D.W. Wynfield, *Coutts Lindsay (1824–1913)*, undated (1860s), albumen print, 202 × 157mm, Royal Academy of Arts.

25 D.W. Wynfield, *James Anthony Froude (1818–1894)*, undated (1860s), albumen print, 200 × 153mm, Royal Academy of Arts.

26 D.W. Wynfield, *Arthur Lewis (1824–1901)*, undated (1860s), albumen print, 219 × 160mm, Royal Academy of Arts.

27 D.W. Wynfield, *John Everett Millais (1829–1896)*, undated (1860s), albumen print, 211 × 162mm, National Portrait Gallery.

28 D.W. Wynfield, *William Holman Hunt (1827–1910), in Tudor costume*, undated (1860s), albumen print, 213 × 163mm, National Portrait Gallery.

29 D.W. Wynfield, *William Holman Hunt (1827–1910), in contemporary dress*, undated (1870s?), albumen print, 212 × 165mm, Royal Academy of Arts.

30 D.W. Wynfield, *Edward Burne-Jones (1833–1898), three-quarters profile*, undated (1860s), albumen print, 211 × 161mm, Royal Academy of Arts.

31 D.W. Wynfield, *Edward Burne-Jones (1883–1898), full face*, undated (1860s), albumen print, 209 × 163mm, Royal Academy of Arts.

32 D.W. Wynfield, *Simeon Solomon (1840–1905)*, undated (1860s), albumen print, 202 × 151mm, Royal Academy of Arts.

33 D.W. Wynfield, *Valentine Cameron Prinsep (1838–1904)*, undated (1860s), albumen print, 206 × 160mm, Royal Photographic Society.

34 D.W. Wynfield, *Frederic Leighton (1830–1896), three-quarters profile*, undated (1860s), carbon print, 192 × 158mm, Royal Academy of Arts.

35 D.W. Wynfield, *George Frederic Watts (1817–1904)*, undated (1860s), carbon print, 211 × 162mm, Royal Academy of Arts.

36 D.W. Wynfield, *Frederic Leighton (1830–1896), full-face portrait*, undated (1860s), albumen print, 213 × 162mm, National Portrait Gallery.

37 D.W. Wynfield, *Edouard Manet (1832–1883)*, undated (1868), albumen print, 216 × 166mm, Royal Academy of Arts.

38 D.W. Wynfield, *William Wetmore Story (1819–1895)*, undated (1860s), albumen print, 213 × 162mm, Royal Photographic Society.

39 D.W. Wynfield, *Alphonse Legros (1837–1911)*, undated (1860s), albumen print, 213 × 163mm, Royal Academy of Arts.

40 D.W. Wynfield, *George Du Maurier (1834–1896)*, undated (1860s), albumen print, 219 × 169mm, Royal Academy of Arts.

41 D.W. Wynfield, *Frederick Walker (1840–1875), full-face portrait*, undated (1860s), albumen print, 195 × 151mm, Royal Photographic Society.

42 D.W. Wynfield, *John Dawson Watson (1832–1892), in falling collar*, undated (1860s), carbon print, 215 × 168mm, Royal Academy of Arts.

43 D.W. Wynfield, *Annie Yeames,* née *Winfield*, undated (1860s), albumen print, 215 × 169mm, Royal Photographic Society.

44 D.W. Wynfield, *Unidentified man*, undated (1860s), albumen print, 212 × 163mm, Royal Academy of Arts.

45 D.W. Wynfield, *Unidentified man*, undated (1860s), albumen print, 213 × 163mm, Royal Academy of Arts.

Select Bibliography

Art Museum, University of New Mexico, *Likenesses: Portrait Photography in Europe 1850–1870*, exh. cat., text by E.A. McCauley, Albuquerque, 1980.

Bartram, Michael, *The Pre-Raphaelite Camera: Aspects of Victorian Photography*, London: Weidenfeld & Nicolson, 1985.

Denvir, Bernard, *A Most Agreeable Society: A Hundred and Twenty-Five Years of the Arts Club*, London: privately printed, 1989.

Dodier, Virginia, 'David Wilkie Wynfield: The Great Amateur', *RA Magazine*, no. 23, Summer 1989, p. 41.

Du Maurier, Daphne (ed.), *The Young George Du Maurier: A Selection of his Letters, 1860–67*, London, 1951.

Du Maurier, George, *Trilby*, 3 vols, London: Osgood, McIlvaine & Co., 1894.

Garner, Margaret, 'David Wilkie Wynfield: Painter and Photographer', *Apollo*, vol. 97, no. 132, February 1973, pp. 158–9.

Garner, Margaret, 'Paintbrushes and Fishing Rods: Summer at Hever Castle', *Country Life*, vol. 168, no. 4332, 28 August 1980, pp. 698–9.

Graham, Ronald, 'Some rediscovered paintings by Great Artists', *Strand Magazine*, vol. 31, no. 185, May 1906, pp. 537–44.

Hallé, Charles, *Notes from a Painter's Life*, London: John Murray, 1909.

The Heatherley School of Fine Art, *The Heatherley School of Fine Art*, text by Rose Eva et al., London, privately printed, 1996.

Hillier, Bevis, 'The St John's Wood Clique', *Apollo*, vols. 79–80, June 1964, pp. 490–5.

Hillier, Bevis, 'Is your family album valuable?', *The Times*, 17 April 1971, p. 22.

International Museum of Photography, George Eastman House, *Cameron: Her Work and Career*, exh. cat., text by Joanne Lukitsh, Rochester, N.Y., 1986.

Jeffares, Bo, *The Artist in Nineteenth-Century English Fiction*, Gerrards Cross: Smythe, 1979.

Leslie, Charles Robert, *A Hand-book for Young Painters*, London: John Murray, 1855.

Leslie, George Dunlop, *The Inner Life of the Royal Academy*, London: John Murray, 1914.

Lukitsh, Joanne, 'Reminders of Titian and Van Dyck: *The Reader* Reviews the Portrait Photographs of David Wilkie Wynfield, 1864', *Victorian Periodicals Review*, vol. 24, no. 2, Summer 1991, pp. 56–63.

Maas, Jeremy, *The Victorian Art World in Photographs*, London: Barrie & Jenkins, 1984.

Marks, Henry Stacy, *Pen and Pencil Sketches*, 2 vols., London: Chatto & Windus, 1894.

May, Colonel H.A.R., *Memories of the Artists' Rifles*, London: Howlett & Son, 1929.

Miriam & Ira D. Wallach Art Gallery, Columbia University, *The Post-Pre-Raphaelite Print*, text by Allen Staley *et al.*, New York, 1995.

Moscheles, Felix, *In Bohemia with Du Maurier*, London: T. Fisher Unwin, 1896.

Prettejohn, Elizabeth, *Rossetti and his Circle*, London: Tate Gallery, 1997.

Reid, Forrest, *English Illustrators of the Sixties*, London, 1928.

Rossetti, Dante Gabriel, 'Hand and Soul', *The Germ*, no. 1, January 1850.

Smith, Mary Stephen, *Art and Anecdote: Recollections of William Frederick Yeames R.A., His Life and Friends*, London: Hutchinson & Co., 1927.

Spencer, Robin, 'Manet, Rossetti, London and *Derby Day*', *Burlington Magazine*, 83, April 1991, pp. 228–36.

Storey, George A., *Sketches from Memory*, London: Chatto & Windus, 1899.

Storey, Gladys, *All Sorts of People*, London: Methuen & Co, 1929.

Surtees, Virginia (ed.), *The Diaries of George Price Boyce*, Norfolk: Real World, 1980.

Taylor, Tom, 'English Painters of the Present Day: D.W. Wynfield', *Portfolio*, vol. 1, 1871, pp. 84–7.

Thackeray, William Makepeace, *The Newcomes* (1855), 2 vols., London: Everyman's Library, 1952.

Unattributed, 'A Brief Enquiry into the Portraiture of Historical Painting', *Art-Journal*, vol. 3, new series, 1 February 1864, pp. 23–4.

Walker Art Gallery, *And When Did You Last See Your Father?*, exh. cat, text by E. Morris and F. Milner, Liverpool: National Museums & Galleries on Merseyside, 1992.

Picture Credits

B.T. Batsford, London: fig. 6
The Bridgeman Art Library, London: fig. 8
National Museum of Photography, Film and Television/ Science and Society Picture Library: fig. 15
National Portrait Gallery, London: figs. 2, 4, 7, 13; pls. 2, 3, 5, 9, 10, 13, 14, 19, 20, 27, 28, 36; back jacket
Private collection: fig. 12
Royal Academy of Arts, London: front jacket; frontispiece; figs: 1, 5; pls. 1, 6, 7, 8, 11, 12, 15, 16, 17, 18, 21, 22, 23, 24, 25, 26, 29, 30, 31, 33, 34, 35, 37, 39, 40, 42, 44, 45
The Royal Collection © 1999 Her Majesty Queen Elizabeth II: fig. 9
The Royal Photographic Society Collection, Bath, England: pls. 2, 4, 32, 38, 41, 43
By permission of the Master and Fellows of St John's College, Cambridge: fig. 14
Photograph courtesy of the Witt Library, Courtauld Institute of Art, London, copyright reserved: fig. 3